MEMORIES FROM A DIFFERENT TIME

RICKY HALBROOKS

seacoast
PUBLISHING

Copyright © 2020 by Ricky Halbrooks

Published by Seacoast Publishing

All rights reserved.

ISBN 978-1-59421-080-8

Cover by Duane Evans

No part of this book may be reproduced in any form or by any electronic or mechanical means, including information storage and retrieval systems, without written permission from the author, except for the use of brief quotations in a book review.

*This book is dedicated to my parents,
Kenneth and Faye Halbrooks.*

CONTENTS

Foreword vii
Ricky Halbrooks

1. ABF — 1
2. Gravel Driveway — 4
3. Smoke Boom — 6
4. Runny Nose Brat — 8
5. I Done the Right Thing — 11
6. Bow Your Head and Close Your Eyes — 14
7. Confusion in a Country Church — 16
8. Kroger — 18
9. Well Wisher — 20
10. Pecan Tree — 23
11. Didn't Hurt — 26
12. Throwing Rocks — 28
13. Blue Hand Boys — 31
14. Egg Hunt (So We Did) — 33
15. Karen's Egg Hunt — 36
16. Reckon Where They're Going — 39
17. TVA Squirrels — 41
18. Old Luke — 44
19. The Hunt — 47
20. Old Luke's puppy is born — 50
21. Spot — 55
22. Squirrel Dog — 58
23. Thanksgiving — 60
24. The Same — 63
25. JDC — 65
26. 98-Pound Weaklin' — 69
27. Basketball — 72
28. First Money — 75
29. My First Gang — 77

30. Tuffy Thompson	79
31. End of Time	82
32. Good Intentions	84
33. When You Hang Out With Trash	86
34. The Jeep	88
35. First Date	91
36. Gas Leak	95
37. Quick Thinking	99
38. Corn Whipping	101
39. I'll Show Them	102
40. Trees and Rocks	105
41. My Mother	108
Epilogue	111

FOREWORD

RICKY HALBROOKS

Hey, you are about to read my stories, which are mostly about events in my life, my friends and family's lives. Hope you enjoy them as much as I enjoyed writing and telling them.

I found early in life telling and writing stories relaxed me and made me happy. It started in school when the teachers would make us write stories using our spelling words. Then the teacher would make you read them in front of the class. Everyone seemed to enjoy mine and would laugh. Then the teachers would always make me read mine first. The teachers, Mrs. Morris, Mrs. Perry and Mrs. Robinson would always encourage me to write. They would tell me you have a great imagination. I would tell them but they are true and we would laugh.

I got asked to leave school the last half of my senior year, which was all right with me. I was already married and working a full-time job. But things were still happening. I was still writing and telling stories.

Me and my wife, Edna, started back to church and dedicated my life to Christ. I became a Lay Speaker for the United Methodist Church. I started speaking for preachers when I was needed. The Lord showed me how to add a little humor in my sermons, and people seemed to enjoy it. I still told stories for people at parties and meetings.

One time I entered a "Whopper Story Telling" contest. There were a lot of people there telling their stories. I came in 3rd place the first time, even though the story I told was true. I got beat by a preacher and a lawyer. A couple of professionals. The next year I came in 2nd. The preacher beat me again.

In 2001, our preacher's mother-in-law, Mrs. Betty, who was from New York and me enjoyed sitting around telling stories of growing up. Mrs. Betty wanted me to enter some of my stories in a writing contest, the National League of American Penwomen Writing Contest. I finally told her I would enter. I entered one story, "Spot", a true story about my dog named Spot. I didn't hear from them for a while. Then one day I got a letter from them. I had won 1st place in non-fiction, the Alabama State Association, 2001 Letters Competition. Boy, I was excited and couldn't wait 'tll Edna got home. (Not to tell her I won, but to ask her what non-fiction meant.) She got home and told me it meant true stories. They called wanting me to send them more stories. I told them not now, maybe when I retire. Me and a lady from Pennsylvania talked for a long time about my story. She really enjoyed it. In 2003, I was put in "The Marquis Who's Who'.

But I got off a little bit. I still write every chance I can. I make copies to give to my friends and kin to read. My mother would read them and save them. She would tell me you should make a book out of these. I would tell her maybe one day after I retire. She would say better do it while I'm still around. Well, she

FOREWORD

passed away before I got these published. I feel like I let her down.

Me in my 1960 Falcon

I hope you enjoy my stories. Most of them are 100 percent true and the rest 98 percent true. I hope you laugh and understand it was a different time. Things were different. I have a lot more to write about. Me and my Uncle Pat sat down one time after he had read some of my stories. We decided they (the stories) were the way I saw them and everybody sees some things different.

My Daddy gave us all nicknames when we were born. Mine was fertilizer. Daddy said because he knew I was full of it. Guess he was right.

I would like to thank Martine Fairbanks and Alice Evans of Seacoast Publishing for working with me to finally get my stories published. I would also like to thank my wife, Edna, for the many hours of typing all of these stories.

Thanks again for taking the time to share in my life stories.

A B F

By the time Marlen, me and David were seven, eight and nine years old, Mom and Dad had 2 more babies, Barry and Karen. Going to town on Saturday was awful. So Mom and Dad would leave us three bigger boys with an older man by the name of Pat Hanley. He owned a lot of land south of Decatur, Alabama. My granddaddy sharecropped the land for Mr. Hanley when Daddy was growing up. They knew each other for a long time. Daddy would drop us off and be gone for three or four hours.

Pat was an old man. We would go to a big shade tree in his front yard and sat down. Mrs. Hanley would bring us milk with ice in it and cookies (tea cake cookies). Pat would start telling us stories (he is probably the reason I like to tell stories now). He told some whoppers. Us boys loved them.

He told about snakes that would rise straight up like a rope plum up to the end of their tail. Rabbits with anthers like a deer, some of them with 6 or 8 points and 2 feet wide! Fish that fly, and birds that can't. The fish would fly right beside the boats. The birds were black and white and they could stay under the water longer than the fish. And frogs, yes frogs, as big as your foot with teeth as sharp as razors. They could jump three or four feet high and are so mean that lions and bears run from them! Us boys believed every word.

One Saturday when Mom and Dad picked us boys up, we were still so excited and laughing we just had to tell them about the stories. About the birds, the fish and snakes, the rabbits and especially the frogs. But instead of getting excited like us, Dad looked back at us and said, "you know them are just tall tales Pat makes up. He has a wild imagination. They are not true." That busted our bubble. We went from excitement to sad. There were no such creatures.

Daddy decided we were old enough to stay at home by our self. We just saw Pat every now and then. But I still remember Pat's stories even though they were just made up.

I got married, went to work installing duct work and units in houses. We had two kids. I was 54- years-old and worked for myself when one day I went with a couple of other men to change a unit in southeast Decatur, on Robinson Street. I drove up, parked, got out and walked up to the front door. But along the way I passed two five gallon buckets covered by boards. Cement block were on top of the boards.

We knocked on the door and the man came to the door. His right hand and arm was bandaged up. One of the fellows knew him and said what have you done to your hand and arm? He grinned and said, "you wouldn't believe it if I told you." Then we went to work. One of my buddies kept telling me, "Ricky, you ought to see what he's got out there in those buckets." But I was up in the attic working and couldn't come down 'til I was done. About dinner I got done and came down. I went and asked the man to show me what was in the buckets. We walked out to the two buckets in the front yard. I got a little worried when he made his kids go inside. He reached down, took the cement blocks off the top of the buckets. He started to take the boards off when he looked up at me and said, "Don't make any sudden move towards them. They will try to take your arm off, like mine." When he uncovered the top of the bucket, there they were, one in each bucket; ABF's—African Bull Frogs! They were as big as my foot and had a full set of sharp teeth. I know this should have scared me, but the only thing that went through my head was "Everything Pat was telling was true!"

My baby pictures

GRAVEL DRIVEWAY

My Father was raised on a farm. His family were sharecroppers. When he turned 18, he went to the Army and fought in World War II. When he came home, Daddy got married, got a job at Decatur Iron & Steel and moved to town, Austinville. Austinville was a part of Decatur, Alabama. Most of the people who lived around us worked at Decatur Iron & Steel or one of the other plants in Decatur, and were fairly equal. There were only three ways you could tell a difference in a family's status. If your house had a paved driveway, you were upper; if you had a graved driveway, you were middle; and if you just drove up beside your house in the yard, you were lower. Of course, we were lower, and not only that, but most of the people had known Daddy all of his life and knew that his family were sharecroppers. They loved to make fun of him by calling him a "hick" or "plow boy." They would tell people he didn't wear shoes 'til he was 13. But one of the funniest was the man who lived behind us and Daddy rode to work with him. He would get up every morning, get on his roof and crow like a rooster. He said it was the only way Daddy would wake up. But none of this really bothered Daddy, he just laughed with them.

Really, Daddy had a lot of common sense and was a very quick thinker. One day us three boys were out in the yard and we had two big sweet gum trees in the front yard so us boys were gathering up sweet gum balls to throw at the neighbor kids. But our neighbor had just got a gravel driveway that day. Us boys were throwing sweet um balls at the neighbors and they were throwing rocks back at us.

When Momma looked out the front window and saw what was going on, she was mad. But about that time, she heard Daddy coming in the back door from work. She went to him, "Kenneth, them boys!" was all she could say. So Daddy started to the living room to go out the front door to see what we were up to. But the phone rang, so he stopped to answer and it was Granddaddy. He asked to talk to us boys. Daddy looked out the window and saw the rock and sweet gum fight. He said to Granddaddy, "the boys can't talk right now, they're busy graveling the driveway." He hung up the phone, opened the front door and yelled out at us, "Boys, move up closer to the road, that's enough rock in that spot!"

SMOKE BOOM

It was early in the morning on the Fourth of July weekend. Me, David and cousins Stanley and Billy, were at our grandmother's apartment in a housing project in Decatur called East Acres. My Aunt Martha Frances, 'old hatchet face,' has been known to pinch a 300 pound bear into submission. One stare from her would make criminals cry and confess. She called mountain lions, "kitty, kitty," and they would come. But us four boys, me, David, Stanley and Billy, had a plan and one smoke bomb left from July 4.

It was hot and the projects had no air conditioning, so Martha Frances left the back door open in the morning while she cooked breakfast. The plan was David would jerk the screen door open, I would strike a match and light the bomb in Stanley's hand, he would throw it into the kitchen where Ma Frances was cooking breakfast, then David would let go of the door, and Billy would prop a stick up on the door so she couldn't get out. Just like in the movies. Then we would go to the alley and laugh at Ma Frances in the smoky kitchen and she couldn't get out. Cousins United. (So that was the plan, I didn't say it was a smart plan).

So David jerked, I lit, Stanley threw, David let go, and Billy propped. But after that things changed. When we got to the alley to laugh, we saw the kitchen full of smoke and learned that propping doors with boards only worked in the movies. Have you ever been in a pasture and looked up to see a big mad bull charging at you? Then you know how we felt when we saw Ma Frances come through the screen door in a rage, charging at us. Cousins United, No! Every cousin for himself. I leaped into the garbage dumpster, Billy went in the back door of Ma Halbrooks' apartment and locked it. David climbed the porch post to the roof and Stanley, poor Stanley, hid in the holly bushes which were full of stickers, spiders and bees.

I say poor Stanley because he was the first one she got. Ma Frances hit the holly bushes, the spiders and bees ran but Stanley didn't. As I laid there in the stink, I heard cries and screams, and could only imagine the pinches and kicks he was taking. But a funny thing, she never got to me, David or Billy. But she put the fear in us through POOR STANLEY.

RUNNY NOSE BRAT

My nose started running about age four and didn't stop until age nine or ten. I started to school at the age of five, because my birthday was in September. I tried my best to keep my nose wiped. My Mom made me wear long sleeved shirts and tote paper towels by the roll in my back pack.

I remember Christmas time in Mrs. Flemmings' first grade class. It started when we drew names and got the person that you drew a gift. I got Tony's name. We got him a cap gun, because he like playing cowboys and Indians. My Mom wrapped it up.

The next day was Friday. We had our Christmas party. Mrs. Flemmings did the party a little different. Each kid got up and told whose name he or she got and what they got that person and why.

Johnny got up and said, "I got Sue's name. Because she loves to color, I got her a big coloring book and colors." She was all smiles.

Then I got up and said, "I got Tony's name and I got him a cap gun because he loves to play cowboys and Indians." "Yea!" Tony yelled. He was happy.

It went on and on. Dolls, cars, trucks, puzzles and games. Gifts for all. We were all excited, especially me! Then it happened. The richest girl in class stood up and said, "I got Ricky's name." All right at last, I thought. "I told my mother whose name I had and she said that little skinny, runny nose brat? We will get him handkerchiefs, a big pack of five and hope he will really use them!"

I was stunned! Everybody was playing and showing off what they got. Everybody but me. I was MAD! So, I went to Tony to get the cap gun back. I was done wrong. Tony didn't like my idea. At 6-years-old, I was pistol whipped by a cap gun (a metal cap gun, not a plastic one).

I took my handkerchiefs home and showed Mom and Dad. They said, "Great you need them." I just cried.

Saturday my brothers found out about the handkerchiefs and it got a lot worse, and Saturday our whole family got together for Christmas. It came time to open gifts. I was excited, let the toys come! But my brothers had heard about school. I opened four gifts, four packs of three handkerchiefs. I looked around at my brothers and cousins playing with there dolls, guns, puzzles and games. I was MAD! So, I ran out and cried and wiped my nose with the long sleeved shirt my Mom made me wear! My brothers and cousins let me play with their toys, but it just wasn't the same as it if they were mine.

Sunday came and our Sunday School Class Christmas party was that night. We had drawn names and I tried to find out who had mine. I had a plan to find out and I would make a deal with them about the gift. I asked all the boys, but none of them had my name. Not any of the girls would talk to me, but the ones I asked said they didn't have my name.

Sunday night came and I was excited. I found out Carolyn had my name and her mother made my gift. I found the box with my name on it, the size of a shoe box. Great! But when it came time to give them out, I opened the box to five more handkerchiefs. Her mother had embroidered my initials (RH) on them. I took them and ran outside. I cried instead of watching everybody else play with their new toys. Now I have twenty-two handkerchiefs and still wearing long sleeved shirts.

Two days later it was CHRISTMAS. I knew, oh yes, I knew what Santa Claus was going to bring me. Me and my brothers always got a model car for Christmas. We got up early, ran down and got our prizes out from under the tree. They were all three just alike. I unwrapped mine. It was a model 55 Chevy. My brothers opened theirs and started putting them together. I opened my box, no car, just three more handkerchiefs. But before I could cry, Mom and Dad came in with the pieces to my car and laughed. I got the glue and started putting my model car together! I was HAPPY!

I DONE THE RIGHT THING

Growing up, my father stressed doing the right thing. He would always tell us boys, "A *man* does what is right, a *boy* does what feels good". But sometimes, as a boy, doing right SUCKS.

It was Christmas 1959, I was 8 years old. My granddaddy Hogan came by and gave me and my brothers, Marlen (9) and David (7), a dollar each for Christmas. When he left Daddy called us boys into the house. Him and Mom had a plan.

He sat us boys down and told us that we were going to Woolworth Department Store. The store had wrapped a bunch of gifts, some were worth a dollar and some more than a dollar. Momma had heard there was a camera wrapped up in the gifts. Momma and Daddy couldn't afford a camera and really wanted one. This trip was a chance to get one for a dollar. So, Daddy sat us boys down and explained we were looking for a box about 6 X 6 and three inches thick. They had looked at them on the store shelves before.

They loaded us up and we took off to Woolworth. When we got there, Daddy asked us boys, "Marlen, Ricky, David, you know what you're looking for, right?" We said "right," and we went into the store and gave the clerk a dollar. She took us over to the Christmas Tree. It was a big old cedar tree with gifts put all around it. Momma and Daddy was watching us close and all excited. Then the clerk said, "One at a time go to the tree and get a gift."

Marlen was first. He walked over like he knew what he wanted; reached down and picked up a gift. But it wasn't no 6X6 three-inch thick box, it was a bag! An eight or ten inch bag! What was he thinking! He walked slowly back, trying not to look at Momma and Daddy. I was thinking, Marlen that's not it! But when he got back to where me and David were, he looked at us and grinned.

David was next. He walked over to the tree, went around it one time, reached down and got a gift – a big gift box about 10 X 16 and eight inches thick. He turned around and started back, he was grinning the whole time. He never made eye contact with Momma and Daddy. I was thinking, "what was David thinking?"

I was next. I walked over to the tree. I was looking hard for the camera box, but what I really wanted was a big round gift, a basketball. Out of instinct I reached down and picked it up, just a-grinning. But when I did, I saw it laying there, a gift about 6 X 6 and three inches thick. Oh me! I put the big round gift down and picked up the little square gift. My grin was gone. As I walked back, all I could think; it's the right thing to do. I looked at Momma and Daddy as I walked back holding up the gift saying, "I think I got it."

We loaded up in the car and went back home. When we got home, we sat in the living room floor to open our gifts. Everyone was excited. Marlen opened his gift first. He tore the

MEMORIES FROM A DIFFERENT TIME

wrapping paper off and guess what it was, army men. A big box of army men, tanks, and jeeps. Just what he'd been wanting!

Next David tore into his and guess what it was . . . a 2-gun holster set. The guns had pearl handles, bullets with straps to tie them to your leg. Just what he always wanted!

Then I opened mine. As I pulled the paper off, there it was in a yellow box with black letters, a KODAK camera. I gave it to Momma, she finished unwrapping it. It was a nice one with film and flash bulbs. Momma and Daddy were tickled to death.

There I sat watching Marlen setting up his army men, lining up his tanks and jeeps. Just a-grinning. There was David putting his guns on and strapping them to his leg. Practicing his quick draw, just a-grinning. Momma and Daddy was loading film, putting bulbs and taking pictures, just a-grinning.

And all I could think was, I could've been dribbling a basketball right now. Doing the right thing SUCKS.

BOW YOUR HEAD AND CLOSE YOUR EYES

My father was a good man. He was a veteran of WWII and believed in rules. For us boys he had two rules that he expressed the most. You say "yes ma'am," "no ma'am," "yes sir" and "no sir" to your elders. You bow your head and close your eyes when people are praying. But when you are six or seven years old there is some things you just got to know, so one Sunday morning sitting in church we all had our heads bowed and eyes closed as the preacher prayed. But curiosity got the best of me, I raised my head and opened my eyes. It was cool! As I looked around everyone had their head bowed and eyes closed – my brothers, my mother, my father and all the other members. So very quietly I bowed my head and closed my eyes. So, I had did it and got away with it. After the preacher said "Amen," the service was over. We got up to leave and as we started to go to the car Daddy grabbed my shoulder, looked at me and said, "Boy you are going to get it when we get home."

"Oh God! If it's possible, come and get me before Daddy gets me home." We didn't live far from the church, but I prayed for divine intervention all the way. When we got home, he said,

"Boy, get in the room." He came in and whipped me. I started crying, but when he started to leave the room, I looked up and said, "How? How?" He said "What?" "How did you know I raised my head and opened my eyes during prayer?" He turned around and looked at me and said, "You did that, too?" He grabbed me and whipped me again.

I never asked him what the first whipping was for, because I learned a good lesson that day. When you do something wrong take your punishment and keep your mouth shut!!!

CONFUSION IN A COUNTRY CHURCH

I was raised way out in the country where the sunshine had to be pumped in. There were seven of us in our family – Momma, Daddy and five kids. We went to an old country church that had an old rock well and the bathrooms outside. It had no air conditioning but it did have electricity and big long fans hanging down from the ceiling. We only had preaching one or two times a month, as we were on a circuit with several other churches. Every Sunday in the summer it was the same thing. We would get to church and there would be only 15 or 20 people there waiting for the preacher to begin his sermon. Someone would turn on the fans and the wasps would start to swarm. One Sunday the preacher began preaching and the funniest thing you would ever want to see happened. There were people slapping, twisting and howling as the preacher was preaching. One person jumped up and ran down to the altar, stung in three places and crying for some water. The preacher was moved and ran down the altar screaming for someone to get some water to baptize this convert. Daddy jumped up and ran to the well, got the bucket, drew some water, ran back into the church and handed it to the preacher. A bucket of water filled with water moccasins! The preacher looked in the bucket and threw it straight up. I guess snake baptism was not his calling. The snakes hit the ground and we all jumped high, slapping and twisting at the swarming wasps, jumping and leaping from the crawling snakes. We were all shouting and howling not wanting to leave till the preacher was done with his sermon. A few days later Daddy was talking to a neighbor who asked what all the shouting was about. Daddy smiled and said, "the Lord sometimes uses the strangest things to get the church a moving."

KROGER

When we were about four, five and six, my brothers, David and Marlen, and me, we didn't have much money and not many chances to get any. Except one day a year at Kroger in Decatur, they would block off about a 20 X 20 foot spot in the parking lot, filled with straw with a lot of change mixed in. Mostly pennies but with nickels and dimes and even quarters mixed in. There were always rumors of half dollars and silver dollars being in there, but we never saw any of those. After they piled the money in the parking lot, they let the kids whose parents were shopping, jump into the straw and find money. They could keep all they could tote out. It became like a competition between me and my brothers, seeing which one of us could tote out the most.

That day came and normally we sat out in the car when Momma was buying groceries, but not today. And normally, we wore shorts, shirts and barefoot. But not today. Today we wore shoes, socks, long pants with pockets and belts, and shirts with pockets. This was the uniforms of the day for the job we had to do. When the time came, we were ready. There were about 20 kids, plus us three, lined up, and ready to jump into the money. Then they started counting off. Get ready! Get set! Go! And off we went, full speed into the pile, grabbing money and stuffing money. Daddy was standing at the car waiting on us. When the man blew the whistle to stop, Marlen was the first out and boy was his pockets full. They were so full they looked like they were about to burst. He had a lot of change. Then I was next, not only did I have my pockets full 'til they were about to burst, but I stuffed my socks with change, put my shirt tail in and stuffed change down my shirt. Boy, I had a whole lot of change! Me and Marlen were grinning from ear to ear. We were loaded with money, more than anybody around. We were sure it was between me and him, so we started counting our money. But then David came out, and he had done it! He put his pants legs inside his socks and stuffed his pants with change, his pants and shirt pockets, but he went even further. As he got to the car, Daddy said, "David what have you done?" David mumbled something and Daddy said, "What are you trying to say, son?" David mumbled again. Me and Marlen said, not really understanding what he said, "Yeah, we know you won." Then David grabbed a jar, opened his mouth and started spitting change in it. Yes, he had even filled his mouth full of money. After he spit it all out, he took a deep breath and said, "What I tried to say, was I think I swallowed six or seven coins!"

David won!

WELL WISHER

Isaac's servants dug in the valley and discovered a well of fresh water there. But the herdsmen of Gerar quarreled with those of Isaac and said, "The water is ours!" So he named the well Esek, because they disputed with him. Then they dug another well, but they quarreled over that one also, so, he named it Sithah. He moved on from there and dug another well, and no one quarreled over it. He named this Rehoboth, saying, "Now the Lord has given us room and we will flourish in the land." (Genesis 26:19-22 NIV)

When I was in the 4th grade, we moved from the town of Austinville to the country near Somerville. We moved from streetlights, paved roads, traffic noise and running water to dark nights, dirt roads, quiet evenings and toting water. While we were building our house, Daddy realized we would need a well for water. This is when I found out that the first person you need when digging a well is not a well digger, but a well-wisher. The first time I saw someone *wishing a well* it was funny and if I saw this being done today, it would still be funny. Daddy found a well-wisher, and a well digger. We were ready to dig a well.

The wisher came early that morning. He was an old man who drove an old truck and used a forked stick to do his job. He grabbed the stick by the forked ends and pointed the straight end in front of him. Everyone was amazed. He walked around the yard muttering to himself, then the stick began to point down. The wisher said to dig at that place. The digger backed his truck up to the spot and began digging. After a few hours, the digger said he had hit rock and not sand rock. The wisher said there was water, and the digger said there was rock.

Daddy said he wasn't paying for this well. The dispute began. They decided to try again. The wisher grabbed his stick and began to wish for water. When he found another spot, the digger began to dig again. After a few more hours, the digger said that he had hit something wet, the wisher said it was water. The digger said it was mud.

Daddy said that we couldn't use mud, and then opposition began. They realized no matter how long they quarreled over it, there was still just mud. We needed water. So, they moved on. The wisher wished for water and found another spot. The digger dug again. After a few hours, the digger shouted that he had found water and that it was a deep, clear well. Daddy said we could use this well! Not only did it furnish us with water, but also sometimes three or four other families would use this well.

As we learn from the scriptures, stay away from disputes, quarreling and opposition for they are not of God. They are life running into rock. They will stop you from going deeper. Like mud, they will cloud your way. But move on where there is none of this for at God's place there is plenty of good, clear water, plenty of Joy, Love, Friendship, Happiness, Grace and room to flourish. Pray, study your Bible, attend your church, love your fellow man and drink the water from the Lord's well.

PECAN TREE

My father worked at Decatur Iron and Steel most of his life. When people would ask him what he did he would say, "I iron all day and steal all night," but he worked hard and made little money. One day he saw a man at work selling shelled pecans a dollar a jar. It seemed like easy money. The tree grows, pecans fall off the tree, you pick them up, shell them, put them in a jar, and sell them. Easy money. He couldn't wait to get home and tell Momma , "We're going to be rich."

So he went out and bought about a two-foot starter pecan tree. He came home and planted it right in front of the house. He watered it every day and put a little fence around it. But he forgot he had kids, five of them, four boys and a girl. But it was a "known rule" you don't mess with the pecan tree.

When we were about 7, 8, and 9, Daddy gave us three older boys a pocket knife. Early one Saturday morning before Momma and Daddy had gotten up, us boys went outside with our knives and were playing a game of stretch. Stretch was a game where you stand about five feet apart and throw your knife at each other's feet. If it sticks up in the ground, the person you threw it at must keep one foot still and stretch the other one to the knife and pull it out before he can throw it back. We hit each other's feet more than the ground. We were screaming and crying, bleeding and fighting. Then Daddy woke up! And Daddy heard what woke him and was mad. He jumped and ran outside. "Boys! Boys! Boys!" He saw what we were doing and when he got to us in the front yard, he reached to get his belt to start whipping boys. But in his anger, he had forgotten his belt, so he grabbed the closest thing he could get his hands on to whip them Boys! And whip he did. But when the dust settled, there he stood, three whipped boys crying and a leafless and broken pecan tree in his hand. "Oh me! Oh me! Oh me! What Have I done to my pecan tree? My dream!" But he replanted it. He babied it, watered it and after a bit it started growing again and getting leaves on it. It was staring to look good again.

When we were about 9, 10 and 11, Daddy got us three older boys a BB gun. Early one Saturday morning before Momma and Daddy had gotten up, us boys went outside with our BB guns. One was at the corner of the house, one was at the pump house and one behind the car. We were having a gun battle. BBs were flying everywhere, boy were we having fun. Until Daddy woke up to the sound of BBs hitting the metal pump house, the metal car, and the glass of his bedroom window. And he woke up mad! He got up running outside, screaming "Boys! Boys! Boys!" When he got to the front yard, he reached for his belt to whip us and realized he had not put his pants on and he had no belt. So in his anger he grabbed the first thing he could get his hands on and started whipping. And whip he did. But when the dust settled, there he stood, three whipped boys crying and a leafless and broken pecan tree in his hand. "Oh me! Oh me! What have I done to my tree? My dream!" But he replanted it, babied it and watered it. After a bit it started growing again and getting leaves again. It was starting to look good again.

In the summer my Daddy and us would go to his brother's house who lived in Georgia on his vacation, and his brother, Don Billy, and his family would come to Alabama to our home on his vacation. Daddy, Momma and us kids were sitting on the front porch waiting for Don Billy and his family to come. In his family was a wife and five kids (five boys). About noon on a hot day, summer day, we sat. Then we saw them coming down the dusty road, flying into our driveway, suddenly stopping. All we seen were car doors opening, dust flying, Don Billy screaming, "Boys! Boys! Boys!" and the boys crying. But when the dust settled, there he stood, Don Billy and five whipped boys crying and a leafless and broken tree in his hand. Daddy jumped up and screamed, "Oh me! Oh me! What have you done?"

Daddy threw away the pecan tree and his dream, faced reality and planted a Weeping Willow tree. It grew to be a very large tree.

DIDN'T HURT

(ZERO CANDY BAR—RC COLA)

When I was growing up in the late 50s early 60s, things were a lot cheaper than now. You could get a 16 oz. RC cola for a dime, and a candy bar for a nickel. Me and my brother David liked to go and get a RC cola and a candy bar every Saturday morning. One Saturday morning we decided to walk to the store and get a RC and a candy bar, but we had no money. So I told David, "we'll have to save our money and wait till next Saturday to get a RC and candy bar." But then a strange look came over David's face (one I had not seen before), then he took his fist and hit me. Then I hit him back. Soon we were in a fight. As soon as Daddy heard the fight, he ran in and said, "Boys! Boys!" Then he grabbed me up and whipped me. Then he grabbed David up and whipped him, then he stormed out. Soon he came back and gave us both a nickel apiece because he felt bad about whipping us. David looked at the nickel and looked at Daddy, then he looked at the nickel again. He looked at Daddy and said, "didn't hurt!" Daddy grabbed us up and started whipping us again, then he stormed out. Soon he came back and gave us another nickel apiece. David looked at the two nickels in his hand, then he looked at Daddy. He looked at the two nickels in his hand again, and then that look came over his face again. I was scared! I had to do something and quick. I reached over and put one of my nickels in David's hand. Then he looked at me and smiled. Daddy walked out.

I feel like my quick reaction saved me from getting beat nearly to death that day. Me and David walked to the store that morning. He got his 16 oz RC and Zero candy bar. I just got a candy bar.

THROWING ROCKS

When I was growing up, we lived way out in the country on a dirt road. We had electric power and lights in our house. We had a phone and an inside bathroom. We had water and in the winter we had running water . . . when we grabbed the bucket and went *running* out to the well pump and came *running* back.

Daddy had our well dug beside our house. Our family and two other families were supplied by the well. Until one day, an old man came to the house. He was an old loner who lived down the road on the side of a hill. He looked mean, dirty and grumpy all the time. He had no electricity. His bathroom was an old, stinky outhouse. His house was an old shack, the drive going to his house was no more than a path. His garden was in his front yard. He had to go a half of a mile to the river to get his water. He had come to our house to ask to get water from our well. Not a lot of people around liked him. My brothers and me didn't like him either. When he knocked on the door, we really didn't want Daddy to answer it, but he did and even asked him in (we didn't know then how hard this was for him to ask for the water). He looked at Daddy and asked if he could get water from time to time. My brothers and I were hoping to hear a "No, and get out." Because we knew what the other neighbors had said. But Daddy smiled, stood up and shook his hand and said, "Yes. You get all the water you need, and you didn't even have to ask." The old man said, "I wouldn't have got any without asking." Then he and Daddy started talking like they had known each other all their lives. My brothers and I listened to every word, not liking this at all. We knew what we would do. We would hide in the woods and throw rocks at him as he walked down the road to our house to get water. We would go at least twenty or so feet into the woods and throw rocks up so they came down on him like rain while he was walking down the road. This went on for a few weeks. The old man never threw rocks back at us or cussed us, and he never told on us to Daddy.

One day coming home, Daddy saw the old man coming down the road with his water can in hand, dodging rocks. Nobody had to tell Daddy anything, he knew what was going on. When we came home, we didn't know Daddy knew, until he said, "Boys, get in the back room!" We knew we were in trouble and we knew why. Daddy was a belt whipper and whip he did. We took our whipping because we deserved it, but what he told us to do next we didn't want to take. Daddy said from now on when we saw the old man getting water we were to go out and help him tote it back to his house. This seemed hard for us boys to understand and soon the day came when the old man came to get water. We knew one of us had to go out and help tote the water back to his house. We decided my oldest brother should go first. Marlen ran out to the pump and said, "let me help you with that." He grabbed one side of the water can. All David and I could think was we hope nobody sees this. When Marlen came back we were waiting. "How bad was it" we asked, but instead Marlen said, "It wasn't that bad, in fact it was kind of interesting." Next it was my time. When the old man came for water I went out and grabbed one side of can and said, "let me help you with that." He said, "okay" and as we walked, we talked. He was quite interesting. He knew about trees, the wild flowers, the rocks and things in nature. When we got to his house, he showed me around. We put up the water and we walked out and saw his garden. When I told him I was going home, he said, "Well, come back sometimes and we'll sit on the front porch and watch the garden growing. Plant life is one of God's miracles too." So I said bye and started home thinking that was interesting. Next it was David's turn. This went on and on until we began looking forward to helping the old man carry his water. The time we visited him became a pleasant learning experience.

If you listen to other people down other people, it will start you downing other people 'til you find yourself throwing rocks at them. But if you give them a chance, or you are made to give them a chance, the people you have been putting down may lift you up.

BLUE HAND BOYS

It was almost Easter and the Easter Egg Hunt was Friday. The teacher decided to tell a little bit about chicken and eggs. It went like this; "the chicken lays the egg in an oval shape, chickens come out of the egg. Remember the Easter Egg Hunt is Friday. Everybody try to bring at least one colored egg"... that was her first mistake - she left out the word BOILED! The way it went was. the poor kids brings one egg, the middle class two eggs and the rich kids three eggs.

We lived out in the country, but were not farmers. We had a pig, a cow and four chickens. There were seven of us and we needed the eggs. The chickens ran around in the yard and they had a place to roost (sleep), a place to lay (eggs) and a place to sit (sit on it's eggs 'til they hatched). Sometimes they sit on up to ten or twelve eggs.

Friday morning came and me and my brother David had no eggs. We went to the kitchen and told Momma we were going to gather eggs. But she said Daddy had all ready gathered them. We looked on the table she had done cooked them (scrambled).

We were desperate! We had to gather some eggs and paint them. Then it came to me, "I got an idea," and told David I will get the eggs. David said, "I have an idea too, I'll get the paint." I ran to the chicken house and David ran to the house.

When I got there, I checked all the laying nests and there were no eggs. So I did it! Yes I did, I went to the setting nest. There she sat. This old hen will flog me to death if I try to get to her eggs. But I was sure going to try! I took my shirt off and then threw it over her head. She tore into my shirt, pecking and scratching it. So while she was doing that, I grabbed six of her eggs and put them in my lunch box. I grabbed my shirt and ran to the bus. Me and David got on the bus and went straight to the back. I opened my lunch box and showed David the eggs. Then David reached in his pocket and pulled out five or six blue ink pen cartridges. We started breaking them open and pouring ink all over the eggs. Ink was everywhere, on our hands, the bus seat, just everywhere! We rolled the eggs around in the lunch box till they were blue and we had six blue eggs for the Easter Eggs hunt (we always told everybody *we* were RICH).

We got to school, we had six eggs (they thought we *were* rich). We had our egg hunt and went back to the classroom. They put all the eggs in a big bowl of water so the mothers who were helping with the egg hunt to shell the eggs for eating – eggs for lunch instead of fish sticks.

Then we heard it. "Yuck! Oh, Oh my God! EEEEEE!" Mrs. Robinson, the teacher, came running in the classroom and shouted, "Who brought the eggs with the chickens in them?" She told the class to raise their hands. We thought it was a test about the chicken and eggs, so we all raised our hands. Then, Mrs. Robinson said, "Everybody but the two boys with blue hands go to the lunch room for fish sticks. You two have an egg bowl to clean!"

EGG HUNT (SO WE DID)

Momma and Daddy never colored or hid eggs at home. But they took us to a lot of egg hunts until people wouldn't let us come to them anymore.

There was three of us boys, me, Marlen and David. I can remember the first egg hunt was at a church, a big church. Named one of them *First* something.

We had our baskets, little wire fruit baskets. We gathered up with all the other kids ready to run out behind the church and find painted real eggs. (We didn't do plastic eggs back then.)

The preacher prayed a little prayer. They said go, so, we did. Boy did we find some eggs. We had eight or nine a piece.

When they said "all right, everybody come on in," we did. When they said, "everybody bring your eggs and let us count them," we did. Marlen gave his eggs to the nice lady and she counted them. "You found eight" the lady said and handed him his basket back. Then she counted mine and the nice lady said, "you found eight," and gave me my basket back. Then she counted David's eggs and the nice lady said, "Oh me, you found ten." Then she gave David's basket back to him.

But David did something that me and Marlen forgot to do. He looked in his basket and seen there were just two eggs in his basket. He looked at the nice lady and yelled at the top of his voice, "You stole my eggs woman!"

Then Marlen looked in his basket and yelled, "You stole six of mine, too!" I looked in my basket and yelled, "you stole six of my eggs!!"

She looked at us and said, "Now, now boys. Everybody gets just 2 eggs. So everyone has the same amount." (All you parents know what we said and loud.)

"That ain't fair!! We want our eggs back."

She said, "No! some kids didn't find but one and some none. This way everyone is even."

David yelled, "I want my eggs back."

The lady said, "Look over there at them kids. They didn't find hardly any."

David looked at the lady, then looked at those kids. A crazy look came on his face. Me and Marlen had seen this face before and knew something was about to happen. David yelled, "I want all my eggs or none." He jumped up on the table and threw his eggs at the other kids. Then me and Marlen started throwing ours. Then the other kids started throwing theirs. We had an all-out egg war. Even one or two hit the nice lady.

The preacher and some other man came running in and broke it up. They escorted me, Marlen and David out, plumb out to the road. There we were – no basket, no eggs and not even a chocolate bunny. We walked home picking egg and egg shells out of our clothes and hair. When we got home, we didn't tell Momma and Daddy nothing about what happened.

The next day, they took us to another church over by East Acres. They were going to have an Easter Egg Hunt after service. My grandmother (Maw) lived there, so after the service Momma and Daddy went over to Maw's house and waited on us. (Bad idea)

We gathered in the fellowship hall with all the other kids. The preacher said a short prayer. A nice lady said, "Go around back and find them eggs." So, we did.

They didn't realize me, Marlen and David didn't have a basket. Yes, we wasn't going to play that game again. We ran to the back yard and all three pulled a paper bag out of our back pocket, and a salt shaker out of our front pockets. We started finding eggs, cracking and shelling them. We threw the shells in the bag as we ate them.

The other kids started watching us. I had ate about four, and Marlen had ate about four. But David had quit trying to find them, he was grabbing them out of the other kid's baskets and shelling, salting and eating eggs right in front of them.

All the kids were screaming, "The Halbrooks are eating the eggs!!! The Halbrooks are eating the eggs!! Come quick. The Halbrooks are eating the eggs!!"

The preacher and some of the other adults broke it up. They told us we wouldn't be welcome back. Then they escorted us out and took us to Maw's house

Word got around about both hunts. Even though we tried, we didn't get to go to any egg hunts anymore.

KAREN'S EGG HUNT

It happened about every other day. Daddy would come home from work and Momma would meet him at the door. "Them boys!!" Daddy would whip us. Then he would say, "You boys stay outside 'til I get home." But we liked watching *Where the Action Is* on TV.

But then Sam came along. Yes, Sam, son of old Luke the best coon dog ever. Sam, the dog no pen could hold. Sam loved to play a game with Momma.

About every other day, Momma would wash clothes and hang them out on the line to dry in the morning. Sam would take them down and when she would come out to bring them in, she would see what he had done. She would get so mad she would meet Daddy when he got home from work. "Kenneth, kill that dog!" Daddy would go running out to the pen and Sam was just sitting there, just grinning at him. Daddy would say, "Sam, stop taking Momma's clothes off the line," then turn around and go back in the house.

Us boys got the break we needed!

After Momma and Daddy had their first baby, a boy name Marlen, they wanted a daughter. When they had another baby, me, the only thing that they carried to the hospital to bring the baby home was a dress. But the baby was another boy, me. After me, there were 2 more boys (David then Barry). Finally, they had a daughter, Karen. Daddy loved his daughter.

When Karen was about 4 years old, Daddy came home from work with a sack in his hand. He handed it to Momma and said, "here's the half dozen eggs and dye for Karen's egg hunt in the morning." "Great, I'll boil them and dye them so you can hide them in the morning for her to hunt," Momma said. "She will love it."

Me and David was listening with our mouths open. What, an Easter Egg Hunt for Karen? We never had that. We had to go out to schools and churches to hunt Easter eggs. But this was all for Karen, the princess.

So, me and David had a plan. That night we slept, one for a little while, and then the other one for a little while, 'til right at day break we heard Daddy in the kitchen getting the eggs and going outside. We went to the bathroom window and watched Daddy hide the eggs. Then we went back to bed and waited for Daddy to go back to bed.

Me and David eased out of bed, went in the kitchen, got a bag and a salt shaker. We went outside. We found all the eggs in just a couple of minutes, cracked, shelled, salted and ate every one of them. We put all the shells in the bags and dumped them in Sam's pen, then turned to sneak back in the house. But for some reason, David tossed his salt shaker in Sam's pen, too. We got in bed and acted like we were asleep.

Daddy and Momma got up, went to get Karen up, and gave her an Easter Basket with a big chocolate bunny, straw and little chocolate eggs. Daddy led Karen outside. But when they got outside there were no eggs. Daddy sent Karen back in the house and told her the Easter Bunny hadn't come yet. He started looking around, then he seen Sam just sitting there in his pen with egg shells everywhere and a salt shaker in his mouth.

Daddy opened the pen door and got the salt shaker out of Sam's mouth, shut the door, turned and went inside. Momma was standing by the sink. Daddy looked at her, handed her the salt shaker, shook his head and said, "That dog! That dog!"

Me and David laid there with egg on our breath! We were thinking we pulled it off. Poor Sam!!

Dad & Family

Thank God that Karen was the caboose And our family was complete. Now we Had to raise them and put them through School.

RECKON WHERE THEY'RE GOING

Our family was first made up of Momma, Daddy, Marlen, Ricky (me) and David. We thought that was it. Daddy gave David the nickname of "Caboose"('cause that was the last box car on the train). Well, about six years later the train changed. Barry and Karen came. Our little *Jim Walter Home* was full!

Me and David slept on bunk beds Daddy had made in the pantry. I slept on the top bunk, David slept on the bottom. There was only enough room to stand and walk in and out. We had to get dressed laying flat on our bed before getting up. Marlen had his own room, cause he was the oldest, the first. Momma and Daddy had their own room also. Barry and Karen slept on the couch in the living room. Barry slept at one end and Karen at the other end. We always said they had the best room in the house, it had a TV and the heater.

When Barry and Karen were about six and five, it happened. One morning while they were still asleep on the couch, Momma had made some more breakfast . . . gravy and biscuits, bacon, sausage, fried eggs, grits and jelly. We were at the table, eating and talking while they slept.

Then we heard something. Daddy looked up, and out the window he saw our 1959 push button drive Plymouth station wagon rolling down the drive with Barry and Karen in the front seat. Daddy looked over at Momma, just as calm as every and said, "Reckon where they think they're going?"

Then we heard a bump and we all went outside. A tree had stopped the car. Barry and Karen was crying. Daddy open the door and asked, "Where's your license?" Then he looked at me and said, "Book them!"

TVA SQUIRRELS

My Uncle Mutt loved to hunt, especially squirrel hunting. We lived out in the country next to Wheeler Wildlife or what we called TVA. Once a year for two weeks they would open the land for hunting, but you had to get a permit. Uncle Mutt called my father up and asked him to get him a permit. Daddy said he would, but he told Mutt that he better remember these were TVA squirrels. TVA squirrels aren't just your everyday wild squirrels. Mutt said he could get them, and laughed. Daddy said, "Okay, but remember I warned you. Be cautious and don't let yourself get tricked. These are TVA squirrels." Mutt laughed and said, "A squirrel is a squirrel. You're just scared I will out-hunt you." Daddy laughed and said, "You've been warned." So Daddy got Mutt a permit.

Soon the open day of the TVA hunt came. Uncle Mutt got there early, way before daylight and he could hardly see his hand in front of his face. He went into the woods a pretty good ways, right next to a creek where he found an old log to sit on and got ready and waited for daylight. He was real quiet. He could hear the sound of the creek, the crickets and the sound of the forest.

But wait! There was some rustling in the trees. There they were, and the trees were full of them. Squirrels! Mutt was excited. There must be at least fifteen of them playing in the trees. He could hear them jumping from tree-to-tree, dropping acorns and mashing the leaves. Mutt couldn't wait till daylight. He was going to get the limit in thirty minutes.

Then, just a few seconds before daylight, everything got quiet. What? What was going on, Mutt thought. Daylight came and there was nothing, not a thing, not squirrel one. What happened? What happened to all the squirrels? Then across the creek one started to move around, way up in the trees. Mutt watched him. Waiting about shooting to see if more would come out. He waited and waited, but there was just the one that came out. Way up in the same tree running back and forth, back and forth all morning.

Mutt was pretty aggravated. He said, "Well, I'm not going back without a squirrel." So he shot at the squirrel across the creek. Boom! He shot the squirrel. Alright, Mutt thought. Got one. But he was across the creek. He had to cross the creek and get it before it got too late. "But my clothes will get soaking wet and freeze" . . . Mutt thought and thought. So he decided he would take off his clothes, cross the creek, dry off with his underwear and t-shirt, put his clothes back on, and go on. So, he took off his clothes, crossed the creek, went to where he seen the squirrel fall at the bottom of the tree. There was nothing but a big pile of leaves. "Where is it? I seen him fall right here," Mutt thought. So he started raking back the leaves looking for the squirrel. But when he raked them to the ground all he found was a hole. Squirrels don't go in holes in the ground, rabbits do that. Squirrels climb trees! About that time, he heard the biggest commotion across the creek, and there he stood, butt-naked looking across the creek at about fifteen or so squirrels carrying off his clothes up into the trees. Uncle Mutt crossed the creek again, got his gun, and started the long walk home. All the way home, Daddy's words kept going through his head, "These are TVA squirrels. They aren't your everyday wild squirrels."

When Mutt got home, he told Daddy what happened with the squirrels. Daddy just laughed and yelled to us at the table, "Hey boys, your Uncle Mutt fell for the old squirrel across the creek trick." Ha! Ha! Ha!

OLD LUKE

Growing up we all hunted. My father trained dogs to hunt; hunt rabbits, birds, squirrels, but mostly he trained coon dogs. He was good at training dogs, but he wanted his dogs to hunt just what they were trained to hunt and nothing else. I've seen him kill or almost beat to death a coon dog for running a rabbit or chasing a squirrel when we were hunting.

He always liked black and tan hounds for coon dogs. He thought they made the best coon dogs. He mostly liked to get the dogs when they were just puppies. He would let them run with the older dogs and they would pick up most of the things to do from them. One thing he did to make them learn to fight and tree coons was to use a pen that was 8 X 8 square with a tree in the center and the bark skinned off. He had us boys go out and catch all the cats we could find whether stray or not. He would put the dog in the pen, take a coon's paw and slap the dog in the face with it till the dog was good and mad. Then he would get out of the pen and tell us boys to start throwing the cats over into the pen, and we would. There would be the worse dog and cat fight you had ever seen or heard – barking, biting, cats crying and scratching. One of us was throwing cats in the pen, and the other two was catching the ones that made it past the dog to the tree where they would jump over the fence. We would catch them and put them back in the bag to be thrown back into the pen. This went on at least an hour or two before Daddy would say stop. By the end of the training us boys always looked the worse – all scratched up, tired, dirty and sweaty. Then we would let the surviving cats go free for another day.

Daddy hunted with a man he worked with called Simp Parker. Simp and Daddy, maybe one or two other men, me and my two brothers, Marlen and David, would hunt the dogs at least two or three times a week. Me and my two brothers were there mostly to carry sacks to put the coons in or to shake the tree or climb the tree and poke the coon out for the dogs to fight, and here too, us boys looked the worse after the hunt. This happened at least two or three times a week 'til the season was over.

Simp had some of the best coon dogs around and of course, Daddy had trained them. But the best coon dog Simp had, and the best I've ever seen, was old Luke. He was a natural. He was the first to tree the coon, and he never lost a fight. Simp and Daddy would take other coon hunters hunting and by the end of the hunt, they would be wanting to buy old Luke. But Simp wouldn't sell.

Daddy and Simp worked at Decatur Iron and Steel. In the winter months, things were really hard and the steel fabrication shop (Decatur Iron and Steel) had no work at all. It was hard to pay bills. Simp came to Daddy and said he was going to have to sell old Luke. The two men were almost in tears. But Daddy said, "Here's what we will do. I have a young female black and tan in heat. We'll breed her with old Luke, have a hunt with a couple of rich business men who coon hunt and sell him to whoever offers the most. We will still have the puppies." Simp and Daddy agreed.

Simp came over with old Luke. He and Daddy put old Luke in the pen with Daddy's female black and tan that was in heat. Old Luke had never been with a female like this before. Old Luke was used to hunting, he hunted with other dogs, but that was it. He had his own pen, his own house, his own traveling pen, his own water and food bowl. Old Luke was getting up in age. Daddy and Simp threw him in the pen with this young aggressive female and left, but us boys didn't leave. Old Luke, the great hunter and the fighter, was about to become the great lover. He didn't know exactly what was going on at first. She would chase him and when he stopped, she would bite him or paw him. Then they would sniff each other's butt. He would go to get a drink, she would go get a drink and push him away. He would go to get some food, she would go there too, then he would run and she would chase him. They would bite and paw, then sniff each other's butt. After hours of this, old Luke finally caught on and animal instinct took control, and the breeding process did happen. And us boys watched it all.

They left poor old Luke in there for about 3 days. He lost about 15 pounds and his eyes were about matted shut. But still when they came to get him, he didn't really seem to want to go, but he did. Simp took him back home to his own pen, his own house, his own food and water bowl. Soon he was looking good again, healthy with his head up and his coat shining. (They did that by feeding him lots of possum.)

THE HUNT

Daddy and Simp had set up the hunt with two of the wealthiest coon hunting business men around. Mr. Sims, who owned the saw mill, and Mr. Sharp, who owned the gin. They had never seen old Luke in action, just heard stories of his great hunts from other hunters, Daddy and Simp.

Simp and Daddy were happy, you could just see the dollar signs in their eyes as the two men pulled up in their new trucks, ready to go hunting. They decided to sell old Luke to one of them. And when the men saw how great a coon hunter and coon fighter old Luke was, they would tell the others about the puppies that were coming, and Daddy and Simp would be rich men.

So Simp and Daddy got the dogs up and then went to get Old Luke. Simp, Daddy, Mr. Sims, Mr. Sharp and all of us boys went into the woods to coon hunt. Everything was going pretty good. Old Luke was looking good. Mr. Sims and Mr. Sharp talked about what a good looking black and tan hound Luke was. Then Daddy and Simp let the dogs loose and old Luke let out a deep piercing bark. Mr. Sims and Mr. Sharp were really impressed, saying what a great sound. Then it happened. Simp reached down to let old Luke join in on the hunt. Daddy looked over at the other two men and said, "We like to turn old Luke out last to give the other dogs a chance." Mr. Sims and Mr. Sharp grinned real big like in anticipation. Simp took off the leash from Old Luke, and Old Luke took off to join the hunt. All four of the men's eyes lit up, "All right, let the hunt begin."

It wasn't long before we heard the worse barking you ever heard. Daddy said, "Simp, what's wrong. That doesn't sound like old Luke, and it doesn't sound like the dogs are treeing anything." The other two men were puzzled. Then Sim said, "I bet Old Luke beat the coon up the tree and is holding him on the ground, keeping the other dogs off 'til we get there to watch the fight." So we all took off to where the dogs were barking. But we didn't get far 'til the dogs met us running back and it wasn't long before we saw why. At the back of the pack was Old Luke. He was running dogs down, male or female, biting, pawing, then sniffing butt!! That night we saw the worse mess of butt sniffing and dog chasing in our life. The last thing on Old Luke's mind was coon hunting – he was chasing, biting, pawing and of course sniffing butt! Simp and Daddy would call Luke; "Come Luke. Luke, get over here!" He would come and start trying to hump on their leg and they would kick him off. He would try to sniff their butt, they would chase him away and he would go after the other dogs. Us boys were laughing our head off. Mr. Sims and Mr. Sharp were, I think, more scared than anything else, saying "Let's go! Let's go!"

Simp and Daddy were beside themselves. What was supposed to be their finest moment had turned into their most embarrassing moment. Not only did Mr. Sims and Mr. Sharp not buy Old Luke, the story of the hunt ruined the sale of any puppies.

I've never seen Daddy and Simp leave a dog in the woods 'til that night, but they did. They gathered up their good dogs and left. That was the last we saw of Old Luke. Yes, the last we saw of Old Luke, he was chasing a deer trying to sniff it's butt. It was about a six-point I believe. Ha Ha! He was probably better off, because Daddy would have shot him for chasing something besides a coon.

OLD LUKE'S PUPPY IS BORN

It wasn't long before the female that Daddy and Simp had bred with Old Luke was ready to have puppies. Simp told Daddy that he could have them. Daddy was trying to think of a way to change the father's name when they came. But the day came and she had the puppy. Yes, the puppy, one was all she had. In a lot of ways, this was okay with Daddy. He thought about going ahead and killing it ending the misery of the Old Luke stories. But he didn't, the puppy was such a fine looking black and tan puppy.

Daddy let us boys name him. We named him Sam. He was an awkward looking puppy, long legs, big feet, little body and long ears that looked like they were twice as big as his head. Sam was a real playful dog, full of energy. I can remember the game him and my mother use to play. Sam would sit in his pen and watch Momma hang out her clothes. When she went back in, he would get out and take all the clothes off the line, sit back at his pen waiting for her to come back out. Sam was the only dog we couldn't keep in a pen. Momma would come out in a rage. "I'm going to kill that dog!" Then we would open the gate and Sam

MEMORIES FROM A DIFFERENT TIME

would run back in, sit and look at Momma like he was saying "you can't get me, I'm on base." Momma would get the clothes up and wash them again. When Daddy would get home from work, he would be met with, "Kenneth, Kenneth, kill that dog. Kill Sam." But for some reason he wouldn't. But Daddy made me and my brothers guard Momma's clothes when she hung them out. Sam would sit and watch us. If we ever left or turned our back for a minute, he was out and the clothes were down.

Soon Sam was old enough to start training to hunt. Daddy put him in the pen with the other coon dogs. Sam seemed okay. He would still get out whenever he wanted to, but he would never go far. Most of the time when we came outside, he would be waiting at the gate to go back in.

Daddy told us boys it was time to get serious about training old Sam. Sam was getting big. He was really big for his age. He was as big or bigger than some of the old dogs. So Daddy told us to go out and catch some cats, and we did. Daddy put Sam in the training pen the day before and we stopped feeding him. Me and my brothers didn't tell Daddy that we had to put Sam back up two or three times because he had got out of the pen. So, Daddy got in the pen, took the coon paw and started slapping Sam in the face with it. Sam got really mad and started biting and lunging at Daddy, knocking him down. When Daddy got to his feet, he jumped out of the pen sand said, "Start throwing them in boys." We did, but Sam was good, those cats never had a chance. Some of the cats never made it to the ground, and none of them made it to the center of the tree or out, even when we threw two or three at a time. It wasn't long before Daddy was shouting, "Stop! Stop!" We did gladly and let the rest of the cats go free. It was awful. They never had a chance. Daddy got Sam out of the training pen. Sam was just sitting there like it was a game. Daddy took him back to the pen. Me and my brothers cleaned up the training pen. Daddy called Simp and some more hunters to tell them what a fighter Sam was, and they couldn't wait to go hunting to see Sam fight.

Soon coon hunting season started. Daddy, Simp (and a couple of hunters, who had embarrassed themselves in front of a hunt before), along with me and my brothers all loaded up the dogs, including Sam, and went hunting. When we got to the woods, Daddy and Simp let all the dogs, even Sam, loose. They took off all together. Soon we heard barking, it didn't sound like they had treed something, but one dog barking and running. So, we stayed where we were and soon we saw what it was. Sam! Sam had a skunk in his mouth running right at us. Simp looked at Daddy and said, "Oh no!" We all turned and ran back to the truck, Sam right behind us. When we got back to the truck, Sam came running up to us trying to show us what he had, and boy did he stink. The two men that was with us jumped in their truck and left, never to hunt with us again. I looked for Daddy to get his gun and kill Sam, but he didn't. Daddy and Simp loaded up all the other dogs, told me and my brother to walk Sam home, stop by the creek and throw him in to try to get some of the stink off of him. So, we did. We were just glad Daddy didn't kill Sam. When we got back home, we put Sam in the pen.

Several days later, Sam got out. He didn't take Momma's clothes off the line, but he ran into the woods, came back with a skunk and stunk up the whole place. Daddy came home and he could smell it, and boy, did it stink. We thought Daddy was going to kill Sam. He seemed useless. He was not allowed to go hunting because he wouldn't run nothing but skunks. When he got out he ran skunks up to the house and stunk up the house. Daddy just turned to us boys and said to wash Sam at the creek then put him back in the pen. So, we did. But this happened again and again, anytime Sam wanted to get or play with a skunk, he would.

MEMORIES FROM A DIFFERENT TIME

Daddy came home one day, Sam had got out and the smell was strong. Daddy told me to go wash Sam in the creek. He and my brothers stayed there and built a special pen for Sam. It was a big pen with a top and bottom to it where he couldn't get out. Me and Sam came back and Daddy said to put him in his new pen. I did, I was just glad he didn't kill Sam. Why he kept saving Sam, I didn't know 'til one evening, we were at home when the phone rang, it was our ring. (We were on a four-party phone line. Our ring was two short rings.) It was my Aunt Martha Frances telling (or warning) Daddy that their cousins from Texas were in and looking for a place to stay. They were rich moochers. They liked to tell you how rich they are, while they stayed in your house and ate your food. They were headed for our house. Daddy said, "Thank you, Sis," hung up the phone and grinned. Momma said, "What is it Kenneth?" Daddy told her who was coming. Momma said, "Oh no, Kenneth, what are we going to do?" Daddy just grinned. In about 15 minutes, we heard a car pull up. It was them. They knocked on the door and Daddy let them in. It looked bad, they had their suitcases in their hands when they came in the door. They sat down on the couch beside the window. Then they started talking or telling us about where all they had been and where they were going, how nice it was traveling in their new Cadillac, and how they hated to leave their big house.

Daddy could see Momma was getting worried. Then Daddy looked over at her and winked. Daddy said, "It sure is hot tonight. I bet y'all got air conditioning in y'all's house, don't you?" They answered, "Well, yes. Our house stays 68 degrees year round." Then Daddy said, "Well, the best we have around here is window fans. We just raise the windows and turn on the fan to pull a breeze through the house." Then Daddy told my brother Marlen to go turn on the fan and he did. Then he turned to me and said, "Ricky, it's time to let Sam out for the night." I looked at him like, what do you mean. Then he said, "Ricky, it's time." So, I did.

Sam wasn't out five minutes before he had a skunk and the fan had pulled the stink all over the house. Daddy's cousins didn't stay long after that, or as Daddy would say later, they left faster than Sam could catch a skunk. They jumped up and said, "We forgot Martha Frances is going to wait up on us!" They grabbed their suitcases, ran to their new Cadillac and left. Daddy just grinned, call Aunt Martha Frances on the phone and said, "Our cousins from Texas are headed your way, and looking for a place to stay."

Then I took Sam to the creek, threw him in, then put him back in his pen. Marlen cut off the fan and Momma sprayed the house with Lysol and lit candles. Daddy just grinned. Then I knew why . . . why Sam was saved, why Daddy didn't kill Sam.

Sam was used many times after this. Daddy even used Sam to breed. His puppies became some of the best coon hunting dogs there ever was. Sam lived a long time, long enough to be called Old Sam (the skunk dog).

SPOT

My father raised and trained dogs, good hunting dogs, when I was growing up. I helped him and learned a lot about training hunting dogs, but my job and what I was trained to do was to kill dogs. Kill stray dogs, sick dogs, dogs that was not here to be trained hunting dogs. I was good at killing other dogs, stray dogs that came around the good hunting dogs' pen trying to get to the hunting dogs' food, or get to them when they were in heat; the sickly dogs or mangy flea bit dogs that could infect our good hunting dogs. I would shoot them in the head and wait a minute to be sure they were dead and when I was sure they were dead, say, "Dog Gone" and walk away. I was good at what I was trained to do.

One day I saw my little brother and his friend on the road. His friend's dog had been hit by a car. When I walked up, they were upset. "Ricky," they said, "What should we do, he's hurt bad." I put the gun to his head. Boom! Boom! Waited a minute, looked up at them and said "Dog Gone" and left them crying over a stupid dog. A few day later Daddy came home and said me and him needed to go over to Ted Terry's house. He had two dogs that I needed to kill for him. They had gotten into a fight and were in pretty rough shape. When we got there, Ted asked what we were going to do, Daddy looked at him and said, "Ricky is going to shoot them." Ted said, "Well, I could do that." Daddy said, "you better let Ricky do it." But Ted wouldn't listen. He went to the pen to shoot them, walked up to them, but was not close enough before he shot them. When he shot the first one, it was not a clean shot, and the dogs jumped up for him and grabbed his leg. He turned and jumped out of the pen. Ted looked at Daddy and said, "What do we do now?" Daddy answered, "Well, I am going to clean up your leg, now Ricky's got to kill them and cut off their heads to take to the vet." Then Daddy turned to me and said, "Do it." I took my gun and ax and did it, because I was good at what I was trained to do. Then we went home.

One day a little long haired, black and white, mangy flea-bit puppy came up, probably one somebody let out to get rid of it. People did that a lot because they couldn't kill them out right, so they let them out in the country to suffer, starve, or get killed by bigger, stronger animals. This little puppy came running up to me. Bark! Bark! Wagging its tail. Most of the time they would have their heads down and their tails between their legs from being beaten and scared. I didn't have my gun to shoot him. Instead of running in and getting it, I looked down at the puppy and said, "Stop, Spot." And he did. When he did sit, he raised one of his paws to me. I reached down and took it. "Good boy, Spot," I said as I smiled and patted the little black and white spotted, mangy, flea bit puppy. I played with him for a good hour or so before I realized I didn't do my job, what I was trained to do. In fact, I couldn't. So, I took Spot a little piece in the woods and tied him on a leash, a rope about 7 or 8 feet long, so Daddy wouldn't know about him.

This was Spot with my sister, Karen. Spot became a family dog.

It was good for a long time. When we treated the hunting dogs' mangy skin with burnt motor oil and sulfur, I would take some out and put some on Spot. His coat was really looking good, and I really enjoyed playing with Spot, he seemed so smart. I remember waking up in the morning, smelling biscuits, gravy, and eggs. My daddy would get up and cook his hunting dogs' breakfast. Us kids would have cereal or oatmeal. I would volunteer to throw out what was left from breakfast. I would really run it out to Spot and stay with him 'til the bus came for school. One night, Spot decided to chew his rope into and came to the front porch looking for me. Daddy jumped up saying, "What is that on the front porch?" He went to the front door and opened it. His first words were, "Ricky, get your gun, there is a stray on the front porch." I got up, walked over to the door and said, "But Daddy, it's just a puppy." "It doesn't matter" he said. "That dog won't hunt." So, I looked at Daddy, then looked at Spot and said, "Stop, Spot," and he did. Daddy looked at me and then I said, "Sit, Spot," and he did. "Shake hands, Spot," and he lifted his paw. I looked at Daddy and said, "Meet Spot. He's my dog." Scared and bold I was, but I loved that dog. Daddy reached down and shook Spot's paw and said, "Welcome to the family, Spot!"

I never had to kill dogs again and it changed Daddy too. Every now and then I would catch him playing with Spot and even giving him some of the breakfast in the mornings.

SQUIRREL DOG

~~~

I grew up hunting. We always hunted. By the time we were 11, 12, and 13, we all had guns. Daddy finally came up one Friday and said, "Boys, get ready. We're going squirrel hunting in the morning. We were excited.

So excited, we got our guns out, cleaned them and got them all ready. Then went to bed, but couldn't go to sleep for nothing. We stayed up all night thinking about squirrel hunting. "I'm going to shoot me some squirrels!"

I finally went to sleep early that morning. The first thing that happens, I heard, "Get up, get ready, get ready." So, we got up and got our guns, and left. We fell in behind Daddy and headed down through the woods, down through Grady Roberts' place.

There Daddy gave each one of us one shotgun shell and said, "When you shoot that shell, bring me a squirrel over to me and I will give you another shell." I thought, "no squirrel, you get no shell. I can deal with that, alright."

Then, he went and sat Marlen down and made sure his gun was on safety. If it wasn't on safety, he took your shell and sent you home.

Then we went a little farther, he sat me down, checked my gun made sure it was on safety. Then Daddy and David went a little ways down. Daddy laid his gun down, that was where he was going to sit. Then he took David down on little bit farther and check his gun, made sure it was on safety.

Daddy made sure we were close to him. Then Daddy, said, "Now boys, listen! We Halbrooks hunt a little different than other people. We give a squirrel a chance. When you see a squirrel, point at it and then shoot it. I was thinking what, I never heard of this, but okay, okay, alright we follow the rules.

So, there we all were sitting and waiting on squirrels to come out. I was thinking, I sure wished I had got up early enough to eat something. Man, I'm hungry. I looked over at Daddy and he was eating a sausage and biscuit. Where's mine?

So, here we were, hungry (except for Daddy) just waiting. Marlen looked up and pointed. We heard BOOM. Then the squirrel fell. Daddy walked over there and got it. He put it in his bag, then went back to his spot.

David was sitting on the other side of Daddy. All of a sudden, he looked up and pointed. The next thing I heard was BOOM! Daddy walked over picked up the squirrel and put it in his bag.

I was sitting there thinking, "Am I the squirrel hunter, or the squirrel dog here? I don't know about this." Then I seen a squirrel. I took off my safety, shot the squirrel and it fell. I walked over there and just before I picked it up, I pointed at it. I took it to Daddy and he put it in his bag.

We were both grinning from ear to ear. He gave me another shell. I was thinking, that is the difference between a squirrel hunter and a squirrel dog.

THANKSGIVING

My father's people always got together on holidays. It would be from 20 to 25 of us most of the time. Our family had seven people, Uncle Billy's had seven people, Maw Frances had three people, Aunt Mildred (who we called Dirty Bird) had three or four, and then there was Maw Halbrooks, Uncle Bobby Ray, and Uncle Pat William. About a week before Thanksgiving Daddy got a phone call from a farmer who lived close to us. The farmer asked Daddy if he would like to help him. He was needing to burn his fields off so he could plow them finer. Daddy said yes, if we could bring our guns and shoot rabbits for Thanksgiving. He told us boys and we started cleaning and getting our guns ready. It would be one of the best hunts we ever had! No going out and buying turkeys. Free rabbits, rabbits, rabbits.

The weekend before Thanksgiving, me and my brothers, Marlen and David, spent Friday and Saturday night at Maw Halbrooks' apartment in East Acres Housing Project, as we did a lot. My two uncles, Bobby Ray and Pat William, lived there too. Us boys liked to hang around Uncle Pat. He was a character of his own. He was conceited and thought he was IT. We loved to watch him primping for hours. He would comb his hair and look in the mirror saying, "Why, why, why did God make me so perfect, so good looking and so irresistible to women?" Then he would look at us and say, "Reckon who is going to be the two luckiest women in Decatur tonight that get to be with Mr. Perfect?" Then he would say, "Boys, I would take one of you with me but the cash is slim. Now I got to get $5.00 from your Grandma and hear her lecture." Me and my brothers were thinking one day we're going to get to go with Uncle Pat. Pat went in and asked Maw for $5.00 to go on a date, and she did lecture him. "Don't you go out and get some little girl pregnant and have to marry her. You don't go and do something stupid like that." She went on and on for about 10 or 15 minutes. Us boys sat and listened, taking in every word. This was an every "date" lecture. It got to be known as the $5.00 lecture. Then Uncle Pat went out on his date and me and my brothers would watch wrestling with my Maw Halbrooks. You have not watched wrestling 'til you watched it with my 69-year-old grandmother. She yelled, jumped and sometimes even threw a chair and other things. We usually spent 10 or 15 minutes cleaning and picking things up after wrestling. We would try to stay up until Pat came in from his date to hear his tales of his night and at the end of the tale he would always say, "Maybe one day I'll have enough money for one of y'all to come along." We would always dream of that day.

After the weekend, we went back home. Monday, Tuesday and Wednesday we went to school. Every evening we would check our guns and count our shells. We were so excited, but no one was as excited as Daddy. He would say, "Rabbits, rabbits, rabbits. Rabbits for Thanksgiving." Thursday morning we got up early. Daddy was already up and waiting for us. Then my uncles, Bobby Ray and Pat William, came up. Then some of the neighbors that were going to help and eat Thanksgiving dinner with us came up. We went to the fields and started the fields burning in the center with one or two of us at each corner. The rabbits started running out. BOOM, BOOM, BOOM! All morning long we shot rabbits, and boy did we get them. We must have had 35 or 40 by about 10 o'clock. The fires were out and Daddy whistled us in from the hunt. We came in with our bags filled with rabbits, rabbits, rabbits. We got home and started cleaning. "Boy, we will have a great Thanksgiving dinner. Not turkey but rabbit, rabbit, rabbit." After we had all the rabbits cleaned and washed, ready for cooking, Uncle Pat came up with a great idea. He told my Daddy his idea. His idea was instead of Mama and the other women having to cook all of them rabbits, he and Marlen would take them to town to Bob Gibson Bar-B-Que and get them to bar-b-que the rabbits. They would be back before the women got the dressing, sweet potatoes and pies ready. Daddy said, "That would be great. Barbecued rabbits for Thanksgiving are even better. Yeah, Pat that is a good idea. You go ahead and get back." Pat and Marlen loaded the rabbits and left. Pat was grinning from ear to ear. Mama and the other women were cooking away. About 6 o'clock everything was ready, on the table and ready to eat. But no rabbits. About 7 o'clock 20 or 30 people were ready to eat and started getting restless and mean. Daddy was walking around saying, "Where are them boys? Where! Where! Where!" . . . I knew. About 8 o'clock, we were having our first vegetable Thanksgiving. It wasn't a happy Thanksgiving, but a quiet one. Pat and Marlen never made it back that night. Later I learned they sold the rabbits, went on their dates and went back to Maw Halbrooks' apartment. I don't remember their punishment, just Marlen grinning. All I remember is me and David were hoping we were next.

THE SAME

When I was young, we were probably considered poor 'til I learned this lesson. We just didn't have a lot of money. My mother made our shirts by hand out of scraps and flour sack material. They fit us just right. We had a small creek behind the house. We swam and played in it even where it was about 8-feet wide and 3 or 4-feet deep. It was cold and clear. In the winter or when times got a little hard, we would eat tomato soup and biscuit puddin' and it was good, us boys would eat biscuit puddin' all the time. We were clothed, had fun and ate good.

But when I was in the 4th or 5th grade in school, a boy came to school, which everybody including himself said was rich. He was a good boy, but as everybody said, his parents had money. A lot of people looked at him differently and a lot of people treated him differently. He became friends with me, my brothers and the boys we hung out with.

One day, he invited us to come home with him to play, swim and eat. Everyone was thinking isn't this going to be special, something different. After school we loaded in his mother's station wagon and went over to his house.

Boy, it was BIG! When we got there, we went up to his room for him to change. When we were up there, he showed us all of his clothes and told us how they were all hand made. Then we went out to go swimming. This was the first house I had ever seen with a swimming pool. It looked nice, but it was about 8-feet wide and 3 or 4-feet deep. It was cool and clear.

We had not been swimming long before his momma called us in to eat. So, we got out of the pool and went in to eat. When we sat down at the table, you can guess what she brought in; tomato soup and for dessert, biscuit puddin'.

Our parents came and got us. When I got into the car. Momma said, "Wow, what a house! They have everything. Now you know how rich folks live." My brother and I looked at each other and said quietly, "Not so different from us."

Rich or poor, things are the same. Rich or poor, God is the same.

JDC

I guess it was my first real bad trouble I got into. It was something dumb, but not the dumbest thing I ever done.

I guess I was about 11-years-old. Me and my little brother, Barry, his friends and my little sister, Karen, and her friends were playing around outside when I heard two shots down in the woods. I saw my brother David and a friend, Roger, come running to the house. They stopped and told me that they were in the woods getting muscadines when the neighbors and the owner of the woods, the Jones' shouted at them to drop the muscadines and get off their land. David and Roger took off running with their bag of muscadines. When one of the Jones' shouted *STOP*, the other pulled out his rifle and shot twice over their heads. But Roger and David ran faster 'til they got home to me. When they told me about the Jones' shooting at them, it made me so mad I told David, "we'll get them."

So, we waited and watched their every move 'til one day when we were sure they were all gone, then me and seven or eight of the neighborhood kids went over there. I made the little ones and my sister, who pitched a fit because I wouldn't let her help, stay on the road and look out for cars coming.

I took a knife and opened the door, or made like I did to look big in front of the other kids (the door was never locked). When we got in, we broke everything breakable and made a mess out of the whole house.

The other kids were all ready out and I was the last one when I saw their rifles hanging on the wall, there was four them. I took them all, went to the back yard and stuck all four guns, barrels first, into the ground. I guess like a message to them. Then we all ran home.

We acted like nothing happened, thinking we were just fine in what we did because they shot at my brother David and at Roger.

The Jones' came home . . . Daddy came home, we never heard a thing. We thought they would call or come over mad, but nothing. They must have got the message and was scared of us or that Daddy would find out they shot at his son. I was the KING. We played anywhere we wanted. Everything was great.

About three weeks had gone by, we had forgotten all about it. Me and my brother David had been down at the river playing and were walking home. When we got close to the house, we saw a big white car in our driveway with the letters JDC in big letters on the doors. Momma was all the time playing them call-in games on the radio. We thought, "all right! Oh Boy! Momma won one on station JDC." We started running fast to the house, and ran in the front door (never reading the fine print under the JDC).

When I came through the door, my first thought was, *radio DJ's in uniforms*? The first words I heard was "Oh, Ricky." Yes, I said really quick, thinking maybe I won. Well, I did, I won a trip in the back of the big white JDC car to the Juvenile Detention Center.

I was scared to death, it was my first of many rides in cars with no back door handles. When we got to Flint where the JDC was, they put me in a room with just a bed. Soon they came and got me and took me to a place like a small court house.

The man asked me if I had broke into the Jones' house. I said, "Yes, Sir." They talked to me and each other for a little while. It was okay, everyone was calm, and so was I 'til he said the words that took me to my knees, begging and crying. The man at the desk asked the officer beside me that deathly question; he said, "Is Ricky's *father* on his way?" That officer said "Yes."

I cried, I begged, "please put me back in the room, lock the door and hide the keys, or shoot me before Daddy gets here. And if you won't do that, open that door and at least give me a running start."

I mean I cried, and I begged, for 10 or 15 minutes. My whole life was flashing in front of me. I was on my knees screaming to the Lord, my God, "if these fellows won't take me, come on and get me before Daddy gets here and sends me to you. Spare me this awful fate that is sure going to be mine."

Then the man behind the desk said, "1 year probation and turn him over to the custody of his parents." Just then my Father came in. The man said, "Mister Halbrooks?" Daddy said, "Yes Sir." The man said, "Ricky is turned over to your custody, take him home." Daddy said thank you. I said "Help! Save me! Anyone!"

I did live, even after a lot of whippings, crying and apologizing to a lot of people.

I think Daddy was the maddest about me using my little sister as a look out. He did talk to the neighbors about shooting over the heads of David and Roger. I guess I should have told Daddy first, and let him take care of it. The neighbor came over and apologized to David and Roger after Daddy talked with them.

98-POUND WEAKLIN'

When I was eleven or twelve, I was about 70 pounds soaking wet, nothing but skin and bones. Life was hard. I was always the first to be picked on by the bullies and the last to be picked or left for teams. Oh, how I wanted to be the big strong one in the bunch instead of just the runt! It seemed the more I ate the less I gained; the more I ran, the whiter and knobbier my knees and legs became. No matter how much weight I would lift, all my arms would do is give, they weren't getting any stronger.

So, I looked around for help to gain size and strength. First one I thought of to ask was the coach. I said, "Coach, will you tell me what to do to make me strong and my muscles big just like yours?" He told me how to make a milkshake of milk, raw eggs and fruit. He said to drink three of these a day and weight you will gain. Then he said to turn all this weight into big and strong muscles, lock your fingers together, then pull and push your feet against the wall.

I left there all fired up to become real big and strong, and I figured it wouldn't take too long. I drank raw eggs and milk but with seven in our family, one a day was all we could afford. I pulled my hands 'til my fingers hurt and pushed my legs against the wall 'til my legs cramped. My knees knotted 'til I could hardly walk.

In just two weeks I lost five pounds and still had white legs and knobby knees. So, I went to the Coach and told him it didn't work. He smiled and said, "For some it do, and some it don't." Then I grinned and said, "I guess I'm the some *it don't*.

There I was a 65-pound weakling, still the first to be picked on and the last to be picked. Life was hard. Oh, what could I do to become big and strong like others I knew. Then one day, while at the magazine stand (looking for pictures of girls and cars), there I saw a magazine of a man who was once just like me. Charles Atlas was his name. It showed a picture of him a 98-pound weaklin' just like me. It told of him going to the beach and the bullies pushing him down and kicking sand in his face. Just like they do me!

So, I got out my money, all I had was 15 cents, and this miracle story book I will buy. All the way home, I read word-by-word how old Charles was a 98-pound weakling that became strong. But when I got to the back, he said, "Buy my product and be strong." This hit me pretty hard, for I spent my only 15 cents to buy his book and to find out how this miracle 98-pound weakling turned strong.

Now he shows a picture of a bunch of springs to pull apart, $14.99 more is all. But that would be hard on a boy so poor. But I decided since I had already invested my 15 cents, I would start saving and the "spring thing" I would get. So, I saved and saved and in just 3 weeks, $10 I had. I wanted this really bad!

Then one day about three weeks before Christmas, to school they came, the Salvation Army. They were telling of children that were so poor that neither fruit or toys these children would get for Christmas to enjoy. These pictures and words broke my heart, so when they passed their cup, my $10 I did stick in so fast that I guess I didn't even think. "Oh, what have I done. I will never be strong!"

So, I thought and thought and decided to just give up and go talk with my Dad. I went to my Dad and told him all about how I wanted to be big and strong. How raw eggs and milk, and pushing and pulling just wouldn't work. So, I tried to buy size and strength through a 15 cent magazine, but they only wanted more. Then I told my father of how I saved and saved to get $10 whole dollars, but when a story of poor children I heard, my weak heart gave my $10 away before my mouth, a word, it could say.

My father smiled down at me and said, "I wish I was the first you came to, the first you came to say how big and strong you wanted to be. I could have told you how big and strong you really are. For being big and tall, with muscles so strong, is just what you can look at, but your heart is where real strength is born. To be chose last and picked on first by man was just worldly ways to try to make you lower than them."

Then my father said, "Even though you came to me last, I had already picked you first on my team. You beat bullies like the devil when you gave from the heart all your $10 to help the poor." Then my father said, "The heart is a muscle that pumps blood throughout, but if Jesus is not in your heart, your body is just dust."

BASKETBALL

(A STAND OUT)

I went to a little country school called Priceville. At Priceville basketball was it. In the 7th grade, I decided I wanted to play basketball. I was about 60 pounds soaking wet and maybe four feet tall. But I thought that it would be the greatest thing to play in a real basketball game.

So, I decided to go out for the basketball team. My buddies had told me, and told me, that basketball at Priceville was for the elite, not for such as me. I said that's okay, but I wanted to play in a real basketball game, so I went out for the team.

At the first tryout I could say I was a real stand out. Everybody had gray shorts and white tennis shoes, but me, the best I could come up with was a pair of daddy's swimming trunks and a $2 pair of Ked's black tennis shoes. There I was, white legs and all. My socks were white socks with blue rings around them.

We lined up and the coach looked us over. Well, he looked over the other boys. But me, he just glanced at and shook his head. It must have been the legs.

Then, we started running. Basketball is a lot of running. The coach really liked me, I could tell because he kept singling me out. I didn't eat a lot of salt, so I didn't sweat a lot. The coach would say everyone runs till Ricky sweats.

Then we practiced shooting, and shooting free shots, or failed shots. Every time you missed a shot, you had to run a lap around the basketball court. I think I might still hold the record of 37 laps for one practice.

These tryouts or practice went on for two weeks. Some boys dropped out, but not many. When it came time to pick the team, there were about eleven boys left. The coach called us to the locker room and said, "Boys, I want you to know I love everyone of you. I have decided that everyone will be on the team." I don't know why everyone looked at me. Maybe it was because I was screaming "yippee" and was grinning from ear to ear! Because I knew that on the 7th grade team everyone gets to play at least one minute in a basketball game.

When they gave out the uniforms, they were beautiful. Gold and black. The coach gave us a pair of nice socks that went over our calves. He wanted everyone to wear white Converse tennis shoes. After practice, I gathered up my stuff and ran home, which was about five miles away.

When I got home, I told my Mother and Father about making the team. I told them about what the coach said. I also told them that we had a game that Friday night. But basketball was not important at our home.

Game day came and I was so excited. But when I started gathering up my stuff and couldn't find my socks. I asked my Mother about them. She said they were too good of socks to play in, I had to save them for Sunday.

When I asked if they had got me some white Converse tennis shoes, she said, "Daddy went to get them but they were $14. That was too much to pay just to play a game in. So, he got some white shoe polish and painted yours."

So, I got my stuff and left for school. Because no matter what, I really wanted to play a real basketball game!

After school, we loaded in the bus and went to Falkville to play basketball. We got there, got dressed and ran out to warm up. As we ran out, the coach looked at us and grinned till he looked at me. He shook his head. Beautiful gold with black trim basketball uniforms and white ankle socks with black rings around the top. White shoe polish on $2 Ked's tennis shoes. We played good that night and won the game.

Oh yes! I got to play in a real basketball game. I was put in the last 3 minutes of the game. I ran out grinning and waving to my buddies that were there. I got in my position and mostly ran around like a chicken with his head cut off.

I was a real stand out. After the game, I told the coach what happened with the shoes and socks. He laughed and said, "I love you. It's okay." I enjoyed that season, and I loved and respected my team mates.

The next season was about to start. The coach called me in his office, looked at me and said, "Let's make a deal." I said, "okay." He asked, "Are you and your brother still working at night?" I said, "Yes." Then he said, "I've talked with the Ag teacher and he's agreed with me – you don't play basketball. You and your brother can go up to the top bleachers and rest, nap or leave early for work. Both of you will pass with a C average." I thought for a few minutes and said, "make it a C+ and you got a deal!" Coach was grinning from ear to ear, "okay!"

FIRST MONEY

I can still remember the first money I ever made or worked for. We never got an allowance or really never knew what it was. If we ever got any money, we walked to the road, picked up coke bottles, cigarettes butts and whiskey bottles with caps on them. We took the coke bottles to the store for the two cent deposit and the whiskey bottles with caps to the bootleggers for five cents. The cigarette butts went to Uncle Pat just to hear him tell us how cool he was.

But then it happened, a farmer about a fourth of a mile away called and asked Daddy if a couple of his boys would like to mow his yard. So, Daddy sent me and my bother David. We were tickled, we were going to make some real money.

We walked to Mr. Buddy Pettit's house. He was a real good man. Mr. Pettit had his lawn mower and about half-acre yard. He showed me and David how to crank the push mower and what to mow. Then we went at it. Tickled to death, we pushed mowed the whole yard as fast as we could and did a real good job. Mrs. Pettit would bring us ice water during the day. Then we were done. We cleaned the grass off the lawn mower and put it up. Mr. Pettit came out, thanked us and paid us a $1.25. It may not sound like much, but to us it was!

But on the way home, we tried to divided the $1.25 in half, and it was always a penny apart. By the time we got home we were in a fist fight. Daddy heard us fighting and came out to see what was going on. "Boys!" Daddy yelled. We came running thinking Daddy will divide this for us. But when we told him what was going on, he took the money and gave it to Mom and said, "this is for you, honey." That made me mad but what he did next, we paid for years to come. Daddy picked up the phone and called Buddy Pettit and said to Buddy, "Thank you for paying my boys for mowing your lawn and they would like to keep mowing the lawn. But pay they can not take."

MY FIRST GANG

In the summer our kin from Georgia came here on their vacation for 2 weeks. They were my Uncle Don Billy, Aunt Fay, and their 5 kids, all boys. Me and my brother David and two of my cousins, Stanley (who we called Boy) and Billy Douglas, were about the same age and we would hang together when they came in. We liked going up to the park at the housing project, East Acres, where my Grandmother Halbrooks lived.

One Saturday me, David, Stanley and Billy walked up to the park to hang out. When we got to the park, there were 2 boys already at the park. We avoided them for a while till they came over and started messing with us, calling us name and cussing at us. One of the boys finally made a mistake; he said his buddy could whip any of us. So I fixed him and said, "I bet he can't whip my brother, David." He said he bet he could, so me and him decided to let them fight and see. We stood around them and they started fighting. David looked pretty good, till the boy hit him again and again. I'm thinking maybe that fellow was right. Then David grabbed him and threw him to the ground, then jumped on top of him. David was looking pretty good till the other boy got on top of David started hitting David again and again. This was about all I could stand; he was starting to hurt David. I looked over at Stanley and nodded at him, he knew what to do. Stanley was always a big boy for his age; he reached over and put the boy standing beside him in a bear hug so he couldn't move. Then I started kicking the boy on top of David. I kicked him in the ribs, in the head, everywhere till he fell off of David. But for some reason I kept kicking him in the ribs and started stomping him in the face. He started to bleed. Billy helped David up and out of the way. Stanley held the other boy in a bear hug. Stanley's boy was turning blue, and my boy was turning red. Then we hear someone calling, "Roger, Roger. Come on home." So I stopped and Stanley let go. They ran about 20 feet away and yelled, "Y'all just come back tonight when my gang is here and try this." I yelled, "We'll be here and take care of them too." Then we started back to Grandma's apartment, feeling good. But when we got in sight of Maw's apartment fear hit me. I saw the line, the bye line. You could tell when Halbrooks were leaving, everybody is in a line hugging and kissing every single kin bye. I looked at Stanley and said, "Y'all aren't leaving are you? Y'all haven't been here but a week." But they were leaving. "Oh my god! This can't be happening." So me, David, Stanley and Billy got in the line. Soon the Georgia bunch, as they were called, were leaving. Everyone was sad and hated to see them go, but no one knew how much David and me hated for them to go.

At dark, me and David walked up to the park. (Smart boys would not have gone) There were 9 or 10 boys waiting on us. We walked up to them scared to death. The boy Roger said we had 2 options. Join the gang or fight. It was the first gang I joined.

TUFFY THOMPSON

I grew up way out in the country about 1/4 mile from the Tennessee River. Me and my brothers would walk down to the river and stay two or three days, fishing and hunting. Momma had made each of us two bags out of flower sacks to wear over our shoulders. One we put taters and carrots in, and the other one we put what we killed or caught in. We had a piece of cardboard to sleep on. We would hunt, fish, swim and have fun. We had a lot of fun and were not afraid of nothing. Sometimes we would come home when it was so dark you couldn't see your hand in front of your face.

But in our family when you turned 14 or 15, you had to get a job and start helping paying bills. So when I turned 15, I went to work at McDonald's in Decatur, Alabama. In the summer I would stay with my grandmother. We called her Maw. She lived in a housing project call East Acres. I started running with some boys from East Acres. East Acres was in the center, Busy Bee was on the east side, apartments were on the south side. Mill Village houses were on the north side. Rich people had houses on the west side. Small apartment buildings were on the east side. We had a rule no one could cut thru East Acres anywhere to get to Busy Bee Grocery Store. You had to go around.

One day we were just hanging out and looked up, and here came a little boy on his bicycle with a sack of groceries. Well, we knew he wasn't from East Acres. First off because he had a bicycle and it had strings of leather straps hanging down from the handle bars. So, when he got to me, I pushed him down, took his grocery bags and threw them in the trash dumpster.

He got up crying, went and got his bags from the dumpster, picked up his bicycle, put his bags in his basket and got back on his bicycle. But before he left he turned and looked me straight in the eyes and said, "Tuffy Thompson is going to get you." Then he grinned and left. I turned around to walk back over to the others. They said, "Oh me, Tuffy Thompson is going to get you."

I said, "What, I'm not scared of anything and I don't know Tuffy Thompson." Then I went in Maw's apartment and got ready for work. I went to work and the boys there said, "We hear Tuffy Thompson is looking for you. He is going to get you." I said, "I don't know, and I'm not scared of no Tuffy Thompson." But all through the night people would come up to me and say, "We hear Tuffy Thompson is going to get you."

When I got off work, I always liked to walk the back alleys to and from work to home, beat on peoples fences to stir up the dogs, making them bark and wake up everybody. But that night was different. They didn't have many street lights back then, but Decatur General Hospital had a big flood light above its door. I got in the middle of the street and ran as hard as I could. I didn't stop 'til I got to that light, then I knew I was safe. (I didn't go down no back alleys).

I rested for just a little while then ran to East Acres to Maw's apartment and started beating on the door. I would knock on the door and Maw would holler, "Who is it?" and I would yell, "It's me, Ricky." Then I would hear her unlocking locks. She had about 4 locks and a chair up against the door. I would say, "It's Ricky" and she would say, "Is that you Ricky?' "It's me, Maw." "Who is it?" "It's Ricky." This went on 'til she got the door opened. I went in, we locked all the locks and put the chair back under the door knob.

Well, the next day came and I stayed in the house all morning 'til time to go to work. I ran to work all the way. I got to work and people was still saying, "Tuffy Thompson is looking for you. Have you seen Tuffy"? This went on for a few days. In fact, it went on for a long time.

I never seen or met Tuffy Thompson. One day I might and then I might get beat up.

But I don't think that would be as bad or change my life as much as the fear a little boy put in my head.

END OF TIME

When I was 15, I started working for McDonald's hamburgers. It brought me many experiences. One God used to help me understand how to look at the end of time.

I worked fries most of the time. Four to nine during the week, four to eleven on Friday, and nine am till twelve midnight on Saturday. One day they brought in a new boy. He was a good boy but not real educated.

Our manager, Mr. B, took him to the time clock and said, "When the big clock hand is on 12 and the little clock hand in on the 5 you begin work. When the big one is on 12 and the little one is on 9 you stop work." Then he took him to the milkshake machine and taught him how to make milkshakes. He showed him how many of each kind to make and keep in the freezer. Mr. B. told him to go to work and he went back to his office.

Alvin, the new boy, started making milk shakes. He was doing good at his job. From where I worked on fries I could see him.

But something bothered him. He would working good, but every 15 or 20 minutes he would run back and look at that time clock. He did this for the first couple of hours. I noticed that the time was on his mind, and Mr. B had noticed it, too. He went to Alvin. I was thinking here comes a chewing, but Mr. B told Alvin, "I want you to understand the time clock, but I want you to do your work when you start. I'll come and get you when it is time to stop.

When we came to Jesus and asked for forgiveness of our sins, our time began and we went to work. His Bible helps us understand His time. It also shows us our work, love, kindness, forgiveness, helping and more. But most of all seeking the lost. I believe Jesus is telling us to understand the time, but do your work. I'll come and get you when it's time to stop.

Acts 1: 6-11

So when they met together, they asked him, "Lord are you at this time going to restore the kingdom of Israel?" He said to them, "It is not for you to know the times or dates the Father has set by His own authority. But you will receive power when the Holy Spirit comes on you, and you will be my witnesses in Jerusalem, and in all Judea and Samaria, and to the ends of the earth." After he said this, he was taken up before their very eyes, and a cloud hid him from their sight. They were looking intently up into the sky as he was going, when suddenly two men dressed in white stood beside them. "Men of Galilee," they said, "why do you stand here looking into the sky? This same Jesus, who has been taken from you into heaven will come back in the same way you have seen Him go into heaven.

GOOD INTENTIONS

I worked at McDonald's from about age 15. The only time McDonald's closed was early Christmas Eve about 6 or 7 p.m. and all day Christmas. They had a Santa Claus who worked the week of Christmas up to an hour before closing on Christmas Eve. Me and my buddy, Tim, worked closing. When we got done cleaning everything, we went to the back room to put our coats on to go home. There it was, Santa's bag full of candy canes. Well, I had 3 brothers and a sister at home. Tim had 4 brothers and a sister at home. We said, "Boy, would they love candy canes on Christmas." So, we started loading our pockets with candy canes. When our pockets were full, we stuffed our shirts and coat sleeves. Then we said bye to the manager real quick, started out the door and down 6th Avenue to Tim's home. We were so happy thinking of how happy our brothers and sisters were going to be.

Then it happened. "Where are you boys going?" A voice said from the car, a police car. We didn't know what to do, run or stay. "Can we talk to you two a minute?" The car stopped and they got out, opened the back door, and said, "Get in." So, we did. Then they said, "Empty your pockets and give us some ID." So, we started pulling candy cane out of our pockets, shirts and sleeves. When the policemen looked back at the back seat, saw all that candy and two teenage boys, they started laughing and laughing. Then they said to each other, "The manager said we would get a laugh out of this." They took us back to McDonald's and we gave the candy back. Even though it was funny, we learned a lesson that Christmas Eve. Wrong is wrong no matter what it is and no matter what our intentions are or how good our intentions are. The road to Hell is paved with good intentions.

WHEN YOU HANG OUT WITH TRASH

When I was a teenager, I spent a lot of my summers with my grandmother in a housing project called East Acres so I could walk to work at McDonald's. It was closer to McDonald's than where I lived in the country. At the housing project I started hanging out with some rough boys. We did a lot of bad and maybe even mean things. It seemed adventurous to a little country boy at that time.

When I got off work at 9 o'clock, the boys would meet me on my way to my grandmother's house. One night we were going to siphon some gas for a car we were planning to steal and hide somewhere for our use. We started in the alleys around Decatur High School because a lot of people parked their cars in their backyard. Things were going okay 'til a back porch light came on and police cars were coming from both ends of the alley. So, we did what any teenage boy would do, we ran. I ran to the back of the school and jumped in a trash dumpster and dug to the bottom. Boy, did it stink . . . boy, was I scared! After about an hour, I was kind of getting use to the smell so I decided to stay another hour to make sure it was clear. After about two hours, I eased out of the dumpster and started to Grandma's house.

When I got to Grandma's house it was 1 o'clock. I went in and Grandma was still up. As I came in, she looked at me, sniffed her nose a little, and said, "You hang around trash, and do trashy things, you end up in trash 'til the smell doesn't run you off." I went to take a bath and go to bed.

What she said didn't make a big difference to me at that time. But later it meant more and more every time I thought of it. As you grow older you realize how smart your parents were, and especially how wise your grandparents were, and how much they loved you.

THE JEEP

When I was still living at home in my teenage years, I had two or twelve cars. Some ran, some didn't. One or two of them you could drive down the road. I spent a lot of my time working on them. That might be why so many of them didn't run. My father would help me and guide me on what to do.

Daddy's only toy was a 1946 Willy's Jeep. My Grandfather Hogan had left it to him when he died. He loved it, he loved to ride and play with it. But us boys was not to touch it (especially me).

One Saturday evening, me and my brother David and some of our buddies were going to go to the drive-in. Me and David were waiting outside when they came up, Rickie and Richie, Winford and Carl. They were in the twins' yellow '57 Chevy ready to go to the show. They were a little early, so we hung out there at the house talking for a while. We decided to take that '57 down the road and see what it would do. So we all got in the car and pulled into the gravel road. Richie was driving, he floored the gas pedal, we took off, and we topped the hill at about 65 mph. I don't know what we were doing at the bottom of the hill, but it was fast. When Richie lost control of the car, we hit the ditch and then went air borne, landing about 20 feet out in the middle of a freshly plowed field. We were stuck in the field. What were we going to do? We were going to miss the show.

Then David said, "Ricky can go up and get the Jeep and a chain to pull us out." Then everybody looked at me. It seemed like a good idea at the time. So I walked the 2 miles back to the house, got the Jeep and the chain. Then went back to pull the '57 Chevy out.

We hooked the chain to the car and to the back of the Jeep. I put the Jeep in 4-wheel low and pulled. It pulled the car right out. But when it did, something went POP. My buddies and brother disconnected the chain. But when I let out on the clutch, the Jeep wouldn't move. They pulled up beside me; I said, "Wait a minute, the Jeep won't move." David said, "What?" I said, "Daddy's Jeep won't move. It's broke and won't move." Then they left! Buddies and brother gone to the show and left me there. I walked the 2 miles back to the house again. I prayed to God for divine intervention.

I decided to just walk in and tell Daddy I broke his Jeep and beg for mercy. So I did, I was scared to death. Daddy stood up looked me in the eyes and said, "Go get in the station wagon and we'll go pull the Jeep home." We got to the Jeep and I was about to cry. He looked at me then looked at the Jeep and said, "This was your granddaddy's Jeep. He was a good and loving man. I know what he would say about this, it's just a material thing, and I love you more than anything you can break or do wrong." He looked me in the eyes and said, "I love you more than a broken Jeep." Then we turned around, hooked up the chain and pulled the Jeep back home.

The Jeep never ran again, but me and him did work on it a lot (maybe that's why). But we spent a lot of time together because of it. I learned this lesson. When our life is broke and won't run, we go to God, He don't condemn us, but tells us, "I love you more. Spend more time working with me."

FIRST DATE

The only reason I was not turned down for many dates was because I didn't ask many out. Love and dating, even having girlfriends, was strange for me. I remember the first girl I asked out was Pam. A pretty little girl with long curly blond hair, blue eyes, big smile and smooth skin. We met several times at the skating rink, McDonald's and other places. She liked to talk, but I was not that much of a talker, and her voice was really whiny and she talked through her nose. But that was okay because she was so pretty to look at, and I looked.

Finally, we decided to go out on a date, a real date. I was to pick her up at six o'clock at her house to go to a party at one of my buddy's house, then we would go eat before going to a walk-in picture show to see a *James Bond* movie.

She had told me her mother was going to school to be a beautician and was going to fix her hair and make-up for our date. I was excited!

I got to her house about 6 o'clock, it was still daylight . . . when she came out and I saw her, my excitement went to horror. "This is not Pam. You go back and get Pam!" But it was Pam!

I don't know what year or what kind of beauty school her mother was going to, but I was sure she was failing and failing badly. She had tried to perm and streak Pam's hair. Something had went terribly wrong. Pam's hair, her long curly blonde hair, now looked like dead grass, brown and dead, and laying flat on her head which made her ears (ears that couldn't be seen before for long curly blond hair) stick out like a couple of catcher's mitts, great big ol' catcher's mitts.

If that wasn't bad enough, the chemicals from her hair got on her hands and in her eyes; her pretty blue eyes were pink with big red veins running all over them and green pus in each corner. I never saw her hands because she had to wear gloves for at least six weeks and not touch anyone.

Then there was the make-up! Thank-you MOTHER! A girl who never wore make-up, a natural beauty, pretty and smooth skin . . . but *this* girl looked like a rodeo clown, Bozo even, except his nose was smaller. The cheap make-up made her nose turn read and swell as big as a baseball, and run like an escaped convict. And her big, big beautiful smile . . . her lips *and* teeth were covered in blood red lipstick, all the way to her chemical blistered tongue. Even with all this you still couldn't help but notice the stitches in her chin, where she busted it when she passed out and fell from smelling the chemicals. I guess her dad did a fair job sewing it up. (He must have been going to "Doctor Tech School"). But it swelled up to the bottom of her neck and turned purple.

Pam jumped in the car and said, "let's go" (but I was thinking, the only way I'm going, is if you pull a gun or knife on me). I said, "Where?" She said, "Out," and smiled, at least I think she smiled, the bright red part of her face that was purple moved. So, we left her house.

There was no way I was going to let my buddies see me with this, so I told her the party was canceled. Then she said,"Let's go eat." No way I was going to be able to eat and look at this. So, I said, "let's wait and get something at the movies." She said, "Okay, but let's go ahead and get a good seat."

Oh my! There is no way I'm walking into the movie with this! So, I drove around till dark, but I think she was getting mad. She said, "I think *James Bond* starts at 8:00." Then I told her we were not going to see *James Bond*, I changed my mind and we were going to see *The Shaggy Dog* at the drive-in (where it was good and dark). She looked at me and said, "The drive in?" Then kinda winked, at least I think she winked, some of her eye lash had fallen off to her chin.

As we drove into the drive-in, I was thinking I may have made a big mistake. We parked, put the speaker in the car window, then I went to get us some drinks and popcorn by *myself*. When I got back to the car about 20 minutes later (I really needed a walk), I jumped in real quick so the light wouldn't come on. I looked at her and I knew she was ready.

Yes, Ready! Ready to start, to start talking; and she made the most whiny-nosed, annoying sound you ever heard. She talked and talked and talked. It was worse than Japanese torture. She talked and she talked, it was one of those sounds that made you sick to your stomach. It was so bad, and I was hurting so bad, that I opened my car door every five minutes, so the light would come on and my eyes would give my ears a break.

Finally, I cracked. I started my car and drove. I didn't even hear the speaker break out my car window as we left.

I took HER, Pam or *whoever* this was, HOME! She never stopped talking and talking. When we got to her house, her mother and father were on the porch. Pam jumped out of the car and screamed, "I never want to see you again!" and ran to her mother and hugged her. As they hugged each other, her mother was looking at me and I was scared, til' her mother grinned . . . GRINNED *and* WINKED, as if this had all went just as she had PLANNED.

GAS LEAK

In 1967 I was sixteen, going to school, and working at McDonald's at night making $1.00 an hour. When you turned fourteen or fifteen in our family, you got a job and started helping pay bills. I understood that, and was okay with it. I paid American Credit and OK Tires. Both of them together were under $40 a month. Everything over that, I put in the bank. My Mom and me went down and started me a savings account with mine and her name on it.

I had three or four cars I was working on. I drove a 1959 Chevy that I owned to work and school everyday, but I really didn't like it.

One day I seen it sitting on a car lot – a 1961 Falcon – a yellow two-door with post between the front and back windows, complete with black roll pleated seats, and a six cylinder with three on a tree (straight shift with gear shift on the column). I wanted it. I went in and talked to the salesman. They wanted $350 dollars and that for me was a lot of money in 1967.

When I got home from work that night, I told Daddy about the Falcon. I told him the price was $350 dollars. I had over $150 in the bank, but I still needed $200 more. Daddy told me to go to American Credit and talk to Mr. Brown.

The next day after school, I went to American Credit and told Mr. Brown about the car. He said hold on just a few minutes, then he went in the back. In about 10 minutes, he came back with a paper in his hand and money in the other.

He told me to come to his office and set down. I did and he showed me the paper. He said, "Ricky, I can not enter in a contract with you because of your age. But I know you and your family and you have always paid the payment. Your Father called and told me what you need and that you might be by. So, this is a friendly agreement."

He showed me the paper. Then he said, "I will give you $200 dollars and you will pay me $21 dollars a week for 10 weeks or till you get it paid off." I said, "great." Then I signed the agreement and took the money.

The next day after school when Daddy got off work, he drove me down to the car lot and I bought the yellow Falcon. I loved it and was happy. I drove it home, but stopped at a hardware store and got six rolls of black tape. I knew what I was going to do with it the minute I had seen the car.

I striped the back of the car from fender-to-fender across the trunk with the black tape like a bee's butt. Then I ran two black tape stripes on the hood from the windshield wipers to the end of the front of the hood like a bee's antennas. It looked like a big bee. I loved that car!

But one night when I got home from work, Daddy was still up and asked me when I came in how I was liking my little yellow Falcon. I said, "I love it except it's not that good on gas as I thought it would be. Every Thursday it's almost on empty. I thought it had a leak, but I checked the gas tank and all the gas line joints. But no leaks."

Daddy thought for a minute then he said, "I tell you what you do. Tomorrow night you park your car in front of the house by the road, then sit out on the porch behind the swing. You and your brother, David, wait there." I said, "wait for what?" He answered, "your gas leak, it will come and you will know it when you see it." I said, "well, okay."

The next night I parked my yellow Falcon in the front yard up close to the road. Me and David sat on the porch behind the swing and waited. We lived way out in the country on Cain Road in Somerville, Alabama, about ¼ mile from the Tennessee River. At night unless the moon is shining it is dark, real dark, and this was a really cloudy night.

We were sitting there and about 12 o'clock, when we heard something, something out by the Falcon. We seen something shiny out there, and someone. I whispered to David, "Go get me my gun and a shell." He went in the house real quiet. I stood up and waited for David. When he came out, I reached over to get the gun and shell, but he had already put the shell in the gun. When he pointed the gun right at the road, I knocked the barrel up a little before he shot. Boom! We seen a gas can go up and somebody pushing a scooter down the road real fast.

Daddy came running out of the house in his underwear. The gun shot hit the house across the road where Horace Draper lived. He came running down the hill in his underwear screaming, "Don't shoot, don't shoot!"

We found a gas can and a piece of water hose. Daddy looked at me and said, "there's your gas leak." We all talked and we knew who it was. "Only one person around has a scooter," and I told Daddy I would take care of it tomorrow.

The next morning, I got up, went out to the Falcon, put the gas can and piece of water hose in my trunk and went to J R Store and filled up with gas. I opened my trunk and filled up the gas can and put the cap back on the can. Then I drove back down Cain Road to where the boy who owned the scooter lived.

I pulled up at the house. People were there but didn't come out. I got out, opened my trunk, got the gas can full of gas and water hose out and put it by the scooter. I put a note on the scooter. It read, "I found your gas can and hose in the road in front of our house. It looked like you spilt all your gas. So I filled it back up for you. P.S. Brother David said he won't miss next time."

My gas leak was fixed.

QUICK THINKING

I always tell about Daddy being a quick thinker in sudden situations, and I like to think that I think quick on my feet. But I have learned quick thinking is not always good, in sudden situations you confirm with your heart too.

Me and my wife, Edna, was married in 1969. The best thing about 1969 thru 1975 was the skirts and dresses were short. My wife was 19 and she wore short skirts and dresses and I enjoyed them very much.

We had to go pick up a friend at the airport who was coming in from New York. I had just got paid and we went by and cashed my check on the way to the airport. I gave it to my wife and she put it in her purse. Every penny we had was in her purse. We got to the airport not long before the plane was to arrive, so we parked at a parking place that had a meter, put a little money in it and went inside. We walked in, then went up a long set of stairs in the middle of the lobby to go where people came in when they got off the plane. People kind of looked at us because I was in my work clothes and she was in a dress, short but not too short. She had brought me some clothes to change into, but we didn't know if I would have time to go ahead and change. We found out what gate our friend's plane was coming into and where to meet her, so we had plenty of time. I told Edna I was going down to the car and get my clothes and change in the men's bathroom in the lobby, then I would come back. Edna said, "Okay, you should have plenty of time."

I went to get my clothes and changed then went to put my work clothes in the car. Right as I was coming in the front doors at the lobby, I looked up and saw Edna coming to tell me our friend's plane was going to be two hours late . . . I was looking and saw it all. Edna had her purse on her arm fixing to go down the steps, when her foot hung in the carpet. There she went head-over-heel down the steps. She hit the bottom of the steps, sunny side up and her purse about ten feet in front of her.

When Edna hit the bottom about five security people in suits came running to her . . . I saw it all. Not five feet away, and now I had to think, and quick. So, I did (this should have told her about my character), I ran over and picked up her purse. Yes, her purse. Then ran over to where she was laying and the security men was helping her. So, I bullied my way thru them and got to Edna, looked at her straight in the eyes, in one of her most embarrassing moments in her life and said, "Here's your purse, lady." I turned and walked away, thinking about how my quick thinking saved her purse and all the money from getting stolen, thinking Daddy would be proud. It wasn't 'til I sat down in the lobby that I realized my quick thinking was about to get me killed, or something worse.

CORN WHIPPING

I always talk about being punished by Daddy, or getting a belt whipping. But I guess each generation tries to make their times seem worse than their kid's. Daddy would tell of the time when they were sharecropping and Granddaddy had them chopping cotton. Granddaddy told him, "Kenneth, run back to the house and get water for us." And he back talked Granddaddy by saying, "No, make one of the girls do it." Well, the corn was green, about three feet tall and had some little hard ears on it. "Oh yeah, you don't talk back to your parents," then Granddaddy looked over at him, walked over to the corn, pulled up a corn stalk, and said, "Kenneth!" Daddy went over to him and Granddaddy started whipping him, or as Daddy put it, whipped him till the ears fell off, either *his* or the corn.

I'LL SHOW THEM

My father was the oldest son of a sharecropping family. There were six kids, four boys and two girls. His daddy worked at Decatur Iron and Steel, so the kids had to do a lot of work in the fields. When my father got older, he felt like he was being used—all of his buddies was getting paying public jobs. He was still working in the fields and his boss most of the time was his mother, relaying what his father said had to be done in the fields . . . 'til he finally said, "I've been used enough, I know what's best for me."

When his daddy got home, he told him, "Daddy, I'm going out to get a job in town." His daddy told him, "No! I need you in the fields and to help your mother at home." Daddy said, "I don't care, I want to make my own money! Mother and my brother and sisters will have to do without me!" His father and mother both begged him not to do this, but the more they talked, the madder he got, 'til finally he stormed out saying, "I'll show them."

When he got to town, he started going from place to place looking for a job, but there were none. He was really starting to get down, when he saw it, *Uncle Sam Wants You* . . . yes, the recruiting office for the army. So, he walked in and joined the U.S. Army in 1943. The recruiter told him to go home, get his things and be back in the morning to get on the bus. Daddy ran back home and told his mother and father about all the money he was going to make in the army. But instead of being happy, they cried and said, "No! Oh no! Son please!" The next day, Daddy was up and gone. His mother and father was still in tears. But all he could think was "I'll show them."

Things went by fast after basic training and the next thing he knew, he was on a ship heading to the Philippines; jumping from island to island 'til he ended up on the island of Guam. Things weren't that bad he thought, "I'm okay, and I'm showing them."

Then one day, they started going out on patrols. He said they went in the jungle early in the morning and it wasn't long till shots came out of the trees. They hit the ground for cover fast. Daddy said there he lay in the mud, soaking wet, scared to death, crying, praying and begging for mercy to the Lord. As he lay there, still as he could, he could hear the wounded crying in pain. All he could remember was his mother crying. He prayed for the Lord's forgiveness like he never knew he could. He begged to see his mother again, that she would never be out of his sight again.

It wasn't long till the fire guns and flame throwers were there. The snipers were burned out. But it felt like forever. Then, they were up and onto the next trail. This happened over and over. It never got any easier and every day he prayed and cried for mercy. Oh, how he longed to see his mother again and how he never would make her cry again. But he never said or thought again, "I'll show them."

Daddy made it through the war and back home. My Uncle Bobby used to tell me of the joy of that day. The day Father saw his mother again.

TREES AND ROCKS

Daddy never made much out of anything he done. He tried to make light of his life. I asked him one time why he went in the Army and came out in the Army Air Corp.

He said, "Son, I joined during war time. A young farmer boy, who'd never been anywhere or did anything. I went to basic training and the next thing I knew, I was on the biggest boat I ever seen with a rifle in my hands, headed to a place I never heard of, the Philippines Islands.

Our first stop was a place called Saipan. It was bad, like I never dreamed of. It was like the Japanese never quit or slept. After there, we went to another Island, Guam. We got there, we got prisoners out of everywhere, out of caves, holes and trees. It was like every tree there was trying to shoot me in the head. I got to hating every tree there. I cried over the dead and the wounded, over and over!

Then I heard they were looking for men to transfer to the Army Air Corp. So, I volunteered. No more trees trying to shoot me in the head. Anything to get off this Island.

This is my Father. Such a young man to go to war.

So, I was in the Army Air Corp. They put me in the back of one of them planes over a gun looking down. The ships looked like rocks on the water. Every one of them was trying to shoot me in the butt. I got to hating every rock."

And we laughed.

When he came home everyone was so happy! But my Aunt Mildred would always tell me he shook so bad he couldn't even hold a coffee cup. I never seen him cry. He said he did enough crying when he was at war. He was a great man. A great father. I was so blessed to be his son.

MY MOTHER

My Mother and Father meet at Flint Methodist Church. Daddy said she made eyes at him. Daddy and his buddy, Cedrick, saw her and both wanted to ask her out. Daddy paid Cedrick a quarter to let him ask her out first. Daddy said it was the best money he ever spent.

She said OK, but most of their dates were at Church. They dated for about four months and married on November 26, 1947.

Momma was beautiful inside and out. I can remember a lot of good times. Momma was a happy person. One time, she got her tickle box turned over and laughed for two weeks. Daddy finally told us kids don't look at Momma for a while. So, we did and after 2 or 3 days she was OK. We must have been real funny looking.

Another time we were living in Austinville. Daddy came in from work and told her we were moving way out in the country. She said, "No! You are not getting me way out in the middle of nowhere with these kids and no way to go."

But we did. We moved way out in Somerville on Cain Road about ¼ mile from the Tennessee River. We could hunt and fish any time.

We had been out there about a month, when one day when Daddy came home from work and seen a fairly new car, a station wagon, in the drive way. He thought, "Oh me, we got company." So, he parked and went in the side door that opened into the kitchen. Momma was standing there cooking. Daddy looked at her and asked, "Who's here?" Momma said, "Nobody." Then he said, "Well, whose car is that?" She said, "Yours and you need to go by McCurry Motors tomorrow to sign papers." He didn't say anything. He did go by and sign the papers.

I can remember when we first moved out on Cain Road we had a well and a bathroom in the house, but no running water in the house. Daddy got us boys, 3 of us, Marlen, Ricky and David. He took us to the bathroom and said, "Boys, you see that toilet and that bucket?" we said, "Yes, Sir." He then said, That's for your Momma. Y'all are to keep that bucket full at all times. If I come in here and it's empty or if your Momma says she came in here and it was empty, I'm gonna to start whipping boys till it's full!"

Then he said, "Follow me." We went to the back door, he opened it and said, "Look out there. You know what that is?" We said, "No." He said, "That, my sons, is three acres of men's rooms. Pick you a spot."

Momma was very special to him and to us. I never heard him raise his voice to her. That was one of the most special thing about my Momma and Daddy, us kids never had any doubt they loved each other.

Momma loved and raised 5 kids in some different times.

I will say this and I don't want it took the wrong way. I love and respected Daddy. I was lucky to have him and think of him a lot.

But I Miss My Mom!!!!

This is Momma. We had a race car at Church for Vacation Bible School. She just had to get inside. The doors didn't open, but she didn't care, she was going to get inside that car even though she had to climb through a window. She was always up for a good time.

This is my Mother in her younger days. She was a beauty.

EPILOGUE

These are just a few of my stories. More to come....

Made in the USA
Columbia, SC
03 April 2024